GALE'S
HONEY
BOOK

GALE'S
HONEY
BOOK

Bridget Jones

Hamlyn

London . New York . Sydney . Toronto

The Story of Honey and *The Gale's Story* by Cliff Lavin

Gale's Honey gratefully acknowledge the assistance given by Mr. N.
Whitehead of the Norwich Bee Keeping Association and Mr. P. E. W. Rodgers,
honey adviser to Colman's of Norwich, during the writing of this book.

Front cover photography by David Johnson
Cover artwork by Robin Lawrie
Illustrations by Joyce Tuhill

Published by The Hamlyn Publishing Group Limited
London . New York . Sydney . Toronto
Astronaut House, Feltham, Middlesex, England
© Copyright The Hamlyn Publishing Group Limited 1983

ISBN 0 600 32384 6

Set in 10 pt Goudy by Tameside Filmsetting Ltd., England
Printed in Italy

Contents

Useful Facts and Figures

Notes on metrication

In this book quantities are given in metric and Imperial measures. Exact conversion from Imperial to metric measures does not usually give very convenient working quantities and so the metric measures have been rounded off into units of 25 grams. The table below shows the recommended equivalents.

Ounces	Approx. g to nearest whole figure	Recommended conversion to nearest unit of 25	Ounces	Approx. g to nearest whole figure	Recommended conversion to nearest unit of 25
1	28	25	11	312	300
2	57	50	12	340	350
3	85	75	13	368	375
4	113	100	14	396	400
5	142	150	15	425	425
6	170	175	16 (1 lb)	454	450
7	198	200	17	482	475
8	227	225	18	510	500
9	255	250	19	539	550
10	283	275	20 ($1\frac{1}{4}$ lb)	567	575

Note: When converting quantities over 20 oz first add the appropriate figures in the centre column, then adjust to the nearest unit of 25. As a general guide, 1 kg (1000 g) equals 2.2 lb or about 2 lb 3 oz. This method of conversion gives good results in nearly all cases, although in certain pastry and cake recipes a more accurate conversion is necessary to produce a balanced recipe.

Liquid measures The millilitre has been used in this book and the following table gives a few examples.

Imperial	Approx. ml to nearest whole figure	Recommended ml	Imperial	Approx. ml to nearest whole figure	Recommended ml
$\frac{1}{4}$ pint	142	150 ml	1 pint	567	600 ml
$\frac{1}{2}$ pint	283	300 ml	$1\frac{1}{2}$ pints	851	900 ml
$\frac{3}{4}$ pint	425	450 ml	$1\frac{3}{4}$ pints	992	1000 ml (1 litre)

Spoon measures All spoon measures given in this book are level unless otherwise stated.

Can sizes At present, cans are marked with the exact (usually to the nearest whole number) metric equivalent of the Imperial weight of the contents, so we have followed this practice when giving can sizes.

Oven temperatures The table below gives recommended equivalents.

	°C	°F	Gas Mark		°C	°F	Gas Mark
Very cool	110	225	$\frac{1}{4}$	Moderately hot	190	375	5
	120	250	$\frac{1}{2}$		200	400	6
Cool	140	275	1	Hot	220	425	7
	150	300	2		230	450	8
Moderate	160	325	3	Very hot	240	475	9
	180	350	4				

Notes for American and Australian users

In America the 8-oz measuring cup is used. In Australia metric measures are now used in conjunction with the standard 250-ml measuring cup. The Imperial pint, used in Britain and Australia, is 20 fl oz, while the American pint is 16 fl oz. It is important to remember that the Australian tablespoon differs from both the British and American tablespoons; the table below gives a comparison. The British standard tablespoon, which has been used throughout this book, holds 17.7 ml, the American 14.2 ml, and the Australian 20 ml. A teaspoon holds approximately 5 ml in all three countries.

British	American	Australian
1 teaspoon	1 teaspoon	1 teaspoon
1 tablespoon	1 tablespoon	1 tablespoon
2 tablespoons	3 tablespoons	2 tablespoons
$3\frac{1}{2}$ tablespoons	4 tablespoons	3 tablespoons
4 tablespoons	5 tablespoons	$3\frac{1}{2}$ tablespoons

An Imperial/American guide to solid and liquid measures

Imperial	American	Imperial	American
SOLID MEASURES		LIQUID MEASURES	
1 lb butter or	2 cups	$\frac{1}{4}$ pint liquid	$\frac{2}{3}$ cup liquid
margarine		$\frac{1}{2}$ pint	$1\frac{1}{4}$ cups
1 lb flour	4 cups	$\frac{3}{4}$ pint	2 cups
1 lb granulated or		1 pint	$2\frac{1}{2}$ cups
caster sugar	2 cups	$1\frac{1}{2}$ pints	$3\frac{3}{4}$ cups
1 lb icing sugar	3 cups	2 pints	5 cups
8 oz rice	1 cup		($2\frac{1}{2}$ pints)

NOTE: When making any of the recipes in this book, only follow one set of measures as they are not interchangeable.

The Story of Honey

Since ancient times man has thought of honey as an almost magical health giver and has used it as a soothing balm and ingredient for alcoholic drinks. Today we recognise honey as nature's finest sweetener, a versatile cooking ingredient and a cosmetic. Yet few people fully understand how it is made. Honey is not just the 'food of the gods' but also the food of the bees, for it is their way of storing precious nourishment to sustain themselves in the winter months. The story of honey is one of nature's most remarkable chapters.

How Honey is Made

There are several species of bee, but it is the honey bee or hive bee (*Apis mellifera*) which is most common and which makes the bulk of the world's honey.

A typical colony of honey bees numbers about 50,000, plus larvae and eggs. The centre of activity is the queen bee, originally a normal larva which the colony has selected and fed royal jelly, a rich, fatty substance, until she grows to a considerable size. The queen lays all the eggs for the hive – up to 2,000 a day! Usually there are some 300 drones or male bees; before the queen is fertilised they are largely idle, and remain in the hive or fly around it making a low buzzing sound – hence the expression 'droning on'! About 25,000 female worker bees remain around the hive, building, repairing, and rearing the young. Another 25,000 older female worker bees act as foragers, travelling up to three miles or more, using their acute sense of sight and smell in search of food for the colony. They are responsible for the production of honey.

Plant nectar, the bee's main food, can be found in flowers, field crops, clover and tree blossom. In addition, bees collect honeydew or manna, a sweet resinous sap found on certain trees. Each plant will provide only a minute amount of nectar, sometimes a fraction of the size of a pin-head. In colder countries the flowering season when nectar is produced is very short. Even though they learn to select the plants richest in nectar, it is estimated that to produce one pound of honey the bees have to travel the equivalent of up to three journeys around the world!

Once a bee has found a suitable plant it draws the nectar up into a honey-sack where it will be mixed with various enzymes. The bee may also collect pollen, kneading it with the nectar to form lumps which are stored in pollen baskets on its rear legs. At certain times of the year the bee will sip minute quantities of water. On returning to its hive the worker bee may perform a remarkable dance to show its companions where nectar can be found. A complex pattern of circles and figures of eight is used to indicate the direction and distance of the plant. The other bees will imitate the dancer bee until they have learnt the pattern and can follow its directions!

The gathered nectar is deposited at the hive in storage cells, and fanned by the worker bees with their wings to reduce its moisture content. As each cell is filled it is sealed up with wax. During mild periods in winter the bees come out of hibernation and break into this store for essential supplies. The pollen the bee has collected is kept separately as the protein supply or 'bee bread' for the young.

Wax is itself a substance of considerable interest, being specially secreted by the bees and chewed before it is put into place as a building material. It has been estimated that bees must consume 16 to 20 pounds of honey for every pound of wax they produce!

The Role of the Beekeeper

In earliest times man used to obtain honey by raiding wild bee colonies; this practice continues today in some under-developed countries. In time he learned to use ladders for reaching nests, and smoke to subdue the bees.

The first hives may have been hollow logs, discarded baskets or clay pots which the bees chanced to settle in. The earliest purpose-built hives were merely an extension of this – a convenient, portable cavity to keep the honey bees close to hand, made out of clay, wicker or wood. In order to extract the honey, the colony, and perhaps even the hive, had to be broken up. The old English conical straw hive or 'skep' was a typical example. This design remained basically unchanged for hundreds of years.

One of the greatest advances in bee-keeping was the adoption of the movable comb hive in the nineteenth century. This was a square wooden hive with vertical trays which could be pulled out either to check the state of the colony or to remove honey. This was made possible by the discovery that bees would respect gaps of one-quarter to three-eighths of an inch in their hive as passages or 'bee spaces'. The interval between trays is so designed that there is just sufficient space to build a comb and leave a bee space; if the gaps were any larger the bees would block them up with wax. Despite this, honey bees have never been domesticated; hive bees are still wild, capable of swarming and leaving to set up new colonies in trees, garden sheds and rafters.

The beekeeper's task is to manage the hive so it produces a quantity of honey surplus to the bees' needs; in autumn or spring he will feed them, to replenish their stores.

The average hive may produce anything from 30 to 90 pounds of honey in a season, depending on the weather and the amount of nectar available. With the reduction in the area of wild land, migratory bee-keeping – moving the hives from one place to another as different flowers and trees come into blossom – is becoming more common. Fortunately, certain modern crops, such as rape-seed, produce a lot of nectar, and indeed can contribute to an extremely delicate flavour. Bees are often rented by fruit growers to help pollinate their orchards in the spring.

Honey in History

From earliest times honey has been highly esteemed by man; prehistoric cave-drawings show the trouble he underwent to obtain it. Interestingly, ancient civilisations used honey as a magical substance, medicine or ingredient in alcoholic drinks, rather than as a food. It was an essential part of many traditions, customs and superstitions, and was often valued as an aphrodisiac!

Some of the best documented evidence for this comes from Egypt, where the bee was one of the Pharoahs' sacred signs. Honey was extensively used in religious rites, including embalming; it was even found in the Pyramids during the twentieth century – still in a recognisable form.

The Ancient Greeks were great honey lovers, believing it essential to a healthy diet. It was an important part of their mythology: 'ambrosia', the food of the gods, was milk and honey, while 'nectar' was fermented honey and spices – mead, in fact.

Britain has long been famed for its honey. The Druids called it 'The Isle of Honey'. For perhaps 2000 years mead was our national drink, until supplanted by beer. Medieval writers strongly approved of it, believing 'there is no drink which conduceth more to the preservation of one', and lamenting that as the English fell to wine and beer 'they were found to be impaired in strength and age'! The word 'honeymoon' is derived from the English custom that the bride and groom should eat only honey and drink only mead for the first four weeks of their marriage.

Bee-keeping in Britain was strongly linked with the demand for beeswax candles in churches, and this declined after the dissolution of the monasteries. The importance of honey as a food was supplanted by the rapid growth of cheap refined sugar from the West Indies. Fortunately Europeans were able to introduce the honey bee to the Americas and Australia, and the vast open spaces of these continents now provide us with a plentiful supply of honey.

Honey for Health

'*My son eat thou honey for it is good*' Solomon in Proverbs

For centuries honey has been used as an ointment, restorative and even elixir of life. Folklore claimed it to be a natural sedative, ideal for relieving tension. It was also thought to promote the correct working of the digestive organs and act as a natural laxative. Much of this is legend without scientific backing; nevertheless, honey has been proved to have some remarkable attributes.

Firstly, it is a valuable source of natural, unrefined sugars, in a form which makes them easily assimilated and it is therefore a favourite food of athletes. The balance of these sugars determines whether the honey is set (crystallised) or clear (runny) and there is no nutritional difference between the two. Both contain traces of minerals, vitamins and amino-acids.

Secondly, honey is a mild antiseptic. It is hygroscopic, drawing water from around it, and thus certain germs cannot survive in it. It is still used in some modern hospitals to aid the healing of burns and wounds.

Honey for Beauty

For centuries honey has featured in the beauty preparations of women all over the world; it is, indeed, one of the oldest recognised natural cosmetics. Its ability to attract and retain moisture means that honey is an effective emollient for the skin and it is perhaps for this reason that so many people consider honey as having magical cosmetic properties.

In practice, honey can be used successfully not only as a softening moisturiser for the skin, but also as an effective hair conditioner. As a cleanser, warmed and smoothed liberally over the face, it attracts the dirt from the pores and helps to clear the skin of blackheads and blemishes. Mixed with other natural ingredients, honey is used in face packs and creams, hair tonics and hand lotions. In fact, it is used quite widely in commercial beauty preparations and particularly in those which rely on only natural products.

Making your own cosmetics is in no way a tedious task. Simply stir together small quantities of readily available natural ingredients to suit your own skin type. The chapter on beauty preparations includes several different types of face pack, a hair conditioner and hand lotion. On its own you will find that warm honey makes an easily rinsed off cleansing agent and mixed with a little single cream it softens the skin to help smooth away wrinkles. For hands, knees, elbows and even feet – wherever you find that your skin becomes rough, then a little honey hand lotion will help.

Once you have tried a few of the beauty treatments collected towards the end of the book, you too will appreciate the soothing goodness of natural honey preparations.

The Gale's Story

R.W. Gale began packing honey and lemon curd in Mortlake, London, around the time of the First World War. The business prospered and moved to larger premises, first in Peterborough in 1951 and finally to Norwich in 1973. Gale's success was built on the mastery of two essentials – selecting and blending.

Selecting honey – the role of the honey taster

Honey can vary tremendously, not only in flavour, colour, and texture but also in quality. If one substandard honey, adulterated, or of poor flavour, is used, it can ruin a whole batch. Despite modern advances in automation this job of quality control still requires a human palate. At Gale's it is performed by an expert honey taster who has spent at least five years perfecting his skill. Every delivery of honey that arrives at Norwich is sampled to ensure that it matches its claimed source of supply and attains Gale's standards of flavour. If not, it is rejected.

The art of blending

Once approved, the honey is carefully examined to determine whether it is best suited for set or clear varieties. Most honey, when collected, is in a runny form but some types have a tendency to become sugary over a period of time, giving a granular texture on the palate. Over the years Gale's has developed a skill in selecting just the right types for either set or clear honey. This helps ensure that set honey retains its consistency and clear honey does not granulate, so each preserves its distinctive character. The honey chosen for the set variety is seeded with existing honey to crystallise it to an even texture. Before bottling, both types of honey are passed through fine cloths to remove any foreign bodies.

The art of blending lies in matching variations in colour, flavour and texture to provide the best result. Considerable experience is required to gauge whether particular flavours and aromas will be complementary. Gale's honey is checked hourly to ensure standards are being maintained.

The result of this care and attention is that Gale's set honey has a creamy texture and reliable consistency ideal for spreading on bread or cooking, while Gale's clear honey keeps for longer without going sugary. Above all, it ensures that both share that richness of taste and aroma loved by generations of Britons.

Honey Cookery

Honey has been valued for centuries in drinks, cakes and desserts. In baking, it can be used to bind ingredients together – pastry and biscuit doughs, for example – while its hygroscopic nature gives moist results and improved keeping quality. The extensive use of honey in savoury cooking is more modern. In fact, its flavour is as important as its sweetening properties, and it will subtly enrich many dishes, such as meat casseroles and savoury sauces.

In this book, the recipes range from starters and main dishes through to vegetable accompaniments, desserts and baking; in addition several of the main courses are suitable for vegetarian meals. Also included are ideas for sweets and drinks. Within each section the dishes cover simple and traditional fare as well as more imaginative ideas and dinner party creations. Throughout the chapters serving suggestions are made and notes on the flavour or texture of unusual foods are given as a guide in menu planning and the presentation of finished dishes.

When you have tried a few of the dishes you will be amazed at the versatility of Gale's honey in cooking. Its unique, distinct flavour can be used with both delicate and full-flavoured foods for incredibly subtle results. Once having experimented, the chances are you will use it more often to enhance your culinary adventures, and with pleasing success.

Starters

The first course of a meal should arouse the appetite for what is to follow. If you are choosing a dinner party menu, first consider your guests and their probable tastes, decide on the main course and then turn your attention to the starter.

Depending on the rest of the meal, the appetiser can be light or rich but never too filling. The dish should be carefully selected and you will find a broad range of ideas to choose from in this chapter. The recipes are either delicate or fairly rich; honey has been used in some cases for its unique flavour, as in the Avocado and Almond Starter, and in others to enrich the result, as in the Curried Cod Kebabs. The Yogurt Cheese Starter is both flavoured and sweetened with honey. Also included are grapefruit and melon ideas, Hot Sweet and Sour Prawns and, for less formal occasions, a peanut dip.

Here we have a selection of dishes which emphasise the versatility of honey in savoury cooking, and guarantee to start off any meal with a touch of flair and imagination.

Avocado and Almond Starter

A warm dressing flavoured with honey and basil emphasises the delicate flavour of the avocado pears in this recipe. To provide interest in the texture, the salad is served on crisp bread croûtes.
Serves 4

Metric		Imperial
4	small thin slices bread	4
2	ripe avocado pears	2
2 tablespoons	olive oil	2 tablespoons
2	shallots, finely chopped	2
50 g	blanched almonds, chopped	2 oz
2 tablespoons	clear honey	2 tablespoons
2 tablespoons	lemon juice	2 tablespoons
1 teaspoon	dried basil	1 teaspoon
	salt and freshly ground black pepper	
50 g	butter	2 oz
	a little paprika (optional)	

Cut the crusts off the bread and set aside. Halve the avocado pears and remove their stones. Peel the halved pears and cut them first into quarters, then into small cubes.

Heat the olive oil in a small pan, add the chopped shallot and blanched almonds. Cook gently, stirring frequently, until the nuts are lightly browned. Stir in the honey, lemon juice and basil and add seasoning to taste. Remove the pan from the heat before adding the prepared avocado.

Melt the butter in a frying pan and add the slices of bread. Turn them almost immediately so that both sides absorb a little of the butter. Continue to fry both sides until they are golden brown.

Drain the slices of bread on absorbent kitchen paper, then transfer them to warmed serving plates. Spoon the avocado mixture on to the bread and serve immediately, sprinkled with a little paprika if you like.

Avocados en Brochette

This is quite an unusual way of serving avocados – the crisp bacon wrapping complements the soft flesh of the fruit and the warm sauce emphasises their delicate flavour. I will cheerfully eat two of these brochettes with a little plain boiled rice and salad for my main course, but they are intended as a starter. Serves 4

Metric		Imperial
1 tablespoon	lemon juice	1 tablespoon
2 tablespoons	dry sherry	2 tablespoons
2 tablespoons	clear honey	2 tablespoons
	dash of light soy sauce	
8	rashers streaky bacon	8
2	large ripe avocado pears	2
	Garnish	
	a few crisp lettuce leaves	
	lemon slices	

Mix the lemon juice with the sherry and honey in a small saucepan. Add the soy sauce and bring to the boil. Simmer gently for 2–3 minutes then keep warm over very low heat.

Cut the rinds off the bacon and cut each rasher in half. Halve the avocados and remove their stones. Peel off the skin and cut each half lengthwise in half again. Cut the wedges of avocado in half to give a total of sixteen chunks. Wrap each piece of avocado in a piece of bacon and thread four on to each of four small metal skewers.

Cook the brochettes under a hot grill, laying them first on a foil-lined grill pan, until the bacon is crisp and brown. Remember to turn the skewers halfway through cooking so that they are evenly cooked.

Arrange the lettuce on four small plates, place a skewer on each and add a slice of lemon. Pour the juices from the grill pan into the sauce and pour this over the brochettes. Serve immediately.

Curried Cod Kebabs

These kebabs make a fairly filling starter. Serve them with
poppadums and a bowl of natural yogurt, sprinkled with a little
chopped fresh coriander and chopped green chillies. Serves 4

Metric		Imperial
450 g	cod fillet	1 lb
1	onion	1
25 g	fresh root ginger	1 oz
2	cloves garlic, crushed	2
2 teaspoons	garam masala (see below)	2 teaspoons
2 tablespoons	clear honey	2 tablespoons
	pinch of turmeric	
	salt and freshly ground black pepper	
	Garnish	
4	large chicory leaves	4
	lemon slices	

Skin the fish (page 19) and cut it into large chunks. Thread these on to four small metal skewers. Peel the onion and the ginger and grate both into a bowl. Add the garlic, garam masala, honey and turmeric. Season generously and stir well to make a paste. Spread this over both sides of the skewered fish.

Cook the fish under a hot grill, turning the skewers frequently, until it is cooked through. This should take about 20 minutes. When cooked the fish will be white through to the middle of each chunk.

Arrange each kebab on a chicory leaf and garnish with lemon slices. Serve immediately.

Garam masala

If you are keen on cooking Indian food you may like to make your own garam masala, as freshly ground spices give a flavour far superior to that which can be achieved by using commercial products.

Roast the following spices together in a dry, heavy-based frying pan over fairly low heat until they give off a pleasant aroma: 1 broken-up cinnamon stick, 1 tablespoon cumin seeds, 2 tablespoons coriander seeds, 3 cardamom pods, 4 cloves and 2 bay leaves. Take care not to overcook the spices or they will become bitter. Cool slightly, then grind to a fine powder and store in an airtight jar.

Hot Sweet and Sour Prawns

These crisp, batter-coated prawns are served with only a small amount of the highly flavoured sauce. As well as making a good starter, they can be served as a main course dish, in which case the recipe quantities should be doubled and the prawns accompanied with plain boiled rice. Serves 4

Metric		Imperial
1 tablespoon	clear honey	1 tablespoon
1 tablespoon	tomato purée	1 tablespoon
1 tablespoon	cider vinegar	1 tablespoon
1	clove garlic, crushed	1
1	small bunch of spring onions, chopped	1
	dash of Tabasco sauce	
	salt and freshly ground black pepper	
100 g	self-raising flour	4 oz
150 ml	water	$\frac{1}{4}$ pint
	oil for deep frying	
225 g	peeled prawns	8 oz
	To serve	
	a few crisp lettuce leaves	

Mix the honey with the tomato purée, vinegar, garlic, spring onions and Tabasco. Add seasoning to taste and set this sauce aside.

Sift the flour into a bowl with a little salt. Gradually beat in the water to make a smooth batter. Heat the oil for deep frying to 180 C/350 F. Dip the prawns in the batter, then drop them into the hot oil and cook until golden brown. Drain the cooked prawns on absorbent kitchen paper.

Shred the lettuce finely and divide it between four small bowls. Pile the prawns on top and spoon over a little sauce. Serve immediately.

Yogurt-dressed Goujons

Serve thinly sliced brown bread and butter with these goujons.
Serves 4

Metric		Imperial
6	plaice fillets	6
	flour to coat	
1	egg, beaten	1
100 g	dry breadcrumbs	4 oz
150 ml	natural yogurt	$\frac{1}{4}$ pint
3 tablespoons	mayonnaise	3 tablespoons
2 tablespoons	clear honey	2 tablespoons
1 tablespoon	tomato purée	1 tablespoon
1 tablespoon	dried oregano	1 tablespoon
	salt and freshly ground black pepper	
	oil for deep frying	
	Garnish	
1	small lettuce, shredded	1
1	small lemon, cut into wedges	1

Skin the plaice fillets (see below) and cut them into strips measuring about 1 cm/$\frac{1}{2}$ in. in width. Coat these fish strips first in a little flour, then in the beaten egg and finally in the breadcrumbs.

Prepare the sauce to accompany the fish before you cook the goujons. Mix the yogurt with the mayonnaise, honey and tomato purée. Stir in the oregano and add seasoning to taste. Pour into a sauceboat or dish ready to serve.

Heat the oil for deep frying to 180 C/350 F. Cook the goujons a few at a time, then drain them on absorbent kitchen paper and keep hot until they are all cooked. Arrange the shredded lettuce in four individual dishes and pile the goujons on top. Garnish with lemon wedges and serve the sauce separately.

To skin fish fillets

Lay the fillets flat on a board with the skin down. Rub your fingers in a little salt and hold the tail end of the fish. (Rubbing your fingers in salt enables you to grip the skin of the fish.) Using a sharp knife, and holding it at a slight angle to the board, cut between the skin and flesh of the fish. Work from the tail towards the head end and cut away from your fingers. Cut fairly slowly using a short sawing motion to avoid breaking the skin at all.

Seafood Pancakes

(Illustrated on page 52)
Yogurt and honey mixed together make a light tangy sauce that goes well with the fish in this tasty pancake appetiser. Serves 4

Metric		Imperial
	Pancake batter	
50 g	plain flour	2 oz
	pinch of salt	
1	egg, lightly beaten	1
150 ml	milk	$\frac{1}{4}$ pint
	a little water	
	butter or oil for frying	
	Filling	
350 g	cod fillet, cooked	12 oz
25 g	butter	1 oz
1	clove garlic, crushed	1
2 tablespoons	finely chopped onion	2 tablespoons
	salt and freshly ground black pepper	
100 g	peeled prawns	4 oz
1 tablespoon	clear honey	1 tablespoon
150 ml	natural yogurt	$\frac{1}{4}$ pint
	Garnish	
	a few whole prawns (optional)	
	sprigs of parsley	

First make the pancake batter. Sift the flour and salt into a bowl. Make a well in the centre and add the egg with a little of the milk. Gradually beat the flour into the wet ingredients, pouring the milk in slowly to make a smooth batter. Add just a little water and leave the batter to stand for 30 minutes.

Meanwhile you can start to prepare the pancake filling. Break the fish into chunks, removing any skin and bones. Melt the butter in a small saucepan, add the garlic, onion and seasoning, then cook gently until the onion is soft but not browned. Remove the pan from the heat and set it aside while you make the pancakes.

Heat a frying pan and grease it lightly with butter or oil. Add a little of the batter and swirl it around to thinly cover the base. Cook until golden brown on the underside, then turn the pancake and cook the second side. Stack the pancakes on a warmed plate, layering absorbent kitchen paper between each to prevent sticking. The batter will make four large or eight small pancakes. Cover and keep them hot in the oven.

To complete the filling, return the saucepan to the cooker and heat until the onion is just sizzling. Add the prawns and honey and stir over low heat until they are hot. Stir in the fish and cook, stirring, for a few minutes. Mix in the yogurt and heat gently without allowing the sauce to boil.

Fill the hot pancakes with the fish mixture, roll them over and serve immediately. Garnish with a few whole prawns, if you like, and a few sprigs of parsley.

Bacon and Mushroom Ramekins

(Illustrated on page 85)
Serve this well-flavoured starter with brown bread and butter or crisp French bread. Alternatively, prepared in one casserole dish, it can be offered with salad for a light lunch or supper. Serves 4

Metric		Imperial
8	rashers smoked streaky bacon	8
1	small onion	1
1	large tomato	1
100 g	button mushrooms	4 oz
1 tablespoon	olive oil	1 tablespoon
1	clove garlic, crushed	1
	salt and freshly ground black pepper	
1 tablespoon	clear honey	1 tablespoon
2	eggs	2
2 tablespoons	dry white breadcrumbs	2 tablespoons
	a little grated Parmesan cheese	

Cut off and discard the rinds from the bacon, then chop it finely. Chop the onion and tomato, then slice the mushrooms.

Heat the oil in a small frying pan, add the onion, bacon and garlic. Season lightly with salt and pepper and cook until the onion is soft. Stir in the honey, mushrooms and tomato and cook for a few minutes. Divide the mixture between four ramekins or individual ovenproof dishes.

Separate the eggs. Beat the yolks with the breadcrumbs and just a little Parmesan cheese. Whisk the egg whites until they stand in stiff peaks and fold into the yolk mixture. Spoon this topping evenly over the bacon and mushroom mixture, then place under a hot grill for a few minutes until browned and crisp on top. Serve immediately.

Yogurt Cheese Starter

Serve this unusual starter with chunks of granary bread or spread like a pâté on wholemeal toast. You may like to mix in the garnish just before it is eaten. Serves 4

Metric		Imperial
	Yogurt cheese	
900 ml	natural yogurt	1¼ pints
	Seasoning and garnish	
1 tablespoon	clear honey	1 tablespoon
1	clove garlic, crushed	1
2 teaspoons	chopped chives	2 teaspoons
5	black olives	5
	salt and freshly ground black pepper	
2	eggs, hard boiled	2
1	56-g/2-oz can	1
	anchovy fillets, drained	

Line a large sieve with a piece of muslin or fine cotton cloth. Pour in the yogurt and gather up the corners. Tie them together and hang the yogurt overnight, placing a bowl under the cloth to catch the liquid that seeps through. Next day the yogurt will have given up all its excess liquid and a creamy 'yogurt cheese' will remain in the cloth.

Mix the honey, garlic and chives into the yogurt cheese. Stone and chop the olives and mix in. Season the mixture to taste, then divide it between four small dishes and chill.

Chop the eggs and anchovies. Arrange these on top of the yogurt cheese and serve immediately.

Yogurt cheese board

A little honey is ideal for taking the edge off the taste of homemade yogurt cheese. Herbs, nuts or spices can be added very successfully, and the cheese can be shaped into a neat round to serve at the end of a meal with Honeyed Oatcakes (page 101).

Sausage and Bacon Rolls

(Illustrated on page 33)
Honey and herbs pep up these old favourites. Hand them around with
drinks instead of serving a more substantial starter. Makes about 24

Metric		Imperial
25 g	butter	1 oz
1	onion, chopped	1
50 g	smoked streaky bacon	2 oz
450 g	pork sausagemeat	1 lb
1 teaspoon	chopped fresh sage	1 teaspoon
1 teaspoon	chopped fresh thyme	1 teaspoon
2 tablespoons	clear honey	2 tablespoons
	salt and freshly ground black pepper	
1	370-g/13-oz packet frozen puff pastry, thawed	1
	beaten egg to glaze	

Melt the butter in a small pan. Add the onion and cook until soft but not
browned. Cut off and discard the rinds from the bacon, then chop it finely.
Mix the fried onion and bacon into the sausagemeat with the herbs and
honey. Season generously.

Roll out the pastry to give an oblong measuring about
25 × 45 cm/10 × 18 in. Cut the pastry in half lengthwise. Divide the
sausagemeat mixture in half and shape each portion into a long roll to lay
down on one piece of the pastry. Dampen the edges of the pastry and fold
over to seal in the filling.

Brush the two long rolls with a little beaten egg and cut each one into
about 12 pieces. Transfer to dampened baking trays and bake in a hot oven
(220 c, 425 f, gas 7) for 15–20 minutes. Cool on a wire rack and serve the
sausage and bacon rolls while they are still warm.

Spiced Peanut Dip

Serve this dip instead of a formal starter or use it as part of a party buffet. Alternatively, it makes an excellent marinade for chicken: pour it over chicken portions and leave to stand for several hours before cooking. Serves 6–8

Metric		Imperial
100 g	salted peanuts	4 oz
1 tablespoon	clear honey	1 tablespoon
2 teaspoons	garam masala (page 17)	2 teaspoons
1	clove garlic, crushed	1
150 ml	natural yogurt	$\frac{1}{4}$ pint

Place all the ingredients in a liquidiser or food processor and blend together until almost smooth. Transfer the dip to a serving bowl and chill before serving with a selection of crisps and crackers, small pieces of fresh vegetable and chunks of cheese or ham.

Minted Melon and Grapefruit Cups

Here is a light summer starter – cool, fruity cups to stimulate the appetite for the meal to come. Serves 4

Metric		Imperial
1	ripe honeydew melon	1
2	grapefruit	2
3–4 tablespoons	clear honey	3–4 tablespoons
4	sprigs of mint	4

Cut the melon in half and scoop out the seeds. Use a melon baller to scoop out the flesh and transfer it to a bowl.

Cut all the peel and pith from the grapefruit, then cut between the segments to remove the flesh. Work over a plate to catch the juice from the fruit. Mix the grapefruit flesh and juice into the melon. Trickle the honey over and add the sprigs of mint. Toss the fruits together and chill thoroughly.

To serve, spoon into glass goblets, carefully picking out the mint to garnish each fruit cup before it is served.

Grilled Grapefruit with Honey and Ginger

Here is a simple and rather old-fashioned way of preparing a grapefruit. As well as making a light first course, this grapefruit goes down well for breakfast on cool mornings when chilled fruit is just too refreshing! Serves 4

Metric		Imperial
2	grapefruit	2
4 tablespoons	set honey	4 tablespoons
	pinch of ground ginger	
2 pieces	preserved stem ginger, diced	2 pieces
4	glacé cherries (optional)	4

Halve the grapefruit then cut between the segments with a serrated, and preferably curved, knife.

Mix the honey with the ground and stem ginger and spread a little over each grapefruit half. Place the fruit under a hot grill, supporting the halves with crumpled cooking foil if necessary, and cook until lightly browned and hot. Serve immediately, garnished with a glacé cherry if you like.

Main Course Dishes

From Marinated Mackerel to Pork Goulash or Aduki Beanpot – these are just a few of the dishes you will find in this chapter. The recipes include imaginative ideas for everyday fare – Sausage and Apple Pie or Smoked Sausage and Chick Peas, for example – as well as some for those occasions when you feel like cooking an extra special meal – Duck with Juniper, perhaps.

There are many well-known meat dishes which require sweetening, such as sweet and sour pork; and when you use honey you are also adding a delicious flavour. In some cases honey is added for contrast – Beef with Chestnuts, for example, combines bitter stout with sweet honey for a rich and flavoursome sauce.

In addition to the many and varied ideas here, don't forget that honey is perfect for glazing even the simplest roast joint – just brush clear honey over pork, lamb and all poultry, then add fresh herbs and plenty of seasoning for superb results. Quite apart from roasts and grills, honey is delicious in vegetarian dishes made from beans and nuts. In fact, the possibilities for using honey in savoury cooking are almost endless!

Marinated Mackerel

This is a deliciously simple way of serving an inexpensive fish. In the summer you can cook this mackerel over a barbecue in the garden – burn some fresh herbs on the coals and they will add an aroma of their own to the fish. Keep the accompaniments to the minimum and serve French bread with a crisp fresh salad to complement this dish.
Serves 4

Metric		Imperial
2 tablespoons	clear honey	2 tablespoons
2 tablespoons	wine vinegar	2 tablespoons
1 tablespoon	mild mustard of your choice	1 tablespoon
	salt and freshly ground black pepper	
4	large mackerel, cleaned	4
4	bay leaves	4

Mix the honey with the vinegar, mustard and plenty of seasoning. Cut the heads off the fish and remove their bones (see page 28).

Lay the fish in a shallow dish and top with the bay leaves. Pour over the marinade and cover with cling film, then place the dish in the refrigerator. Leave the fish to marinate for several hours or overnight.

Cook the fish opened out under a hot grill, basting frequently with the marinade, until it is cooked through. The cooking time will depend on the size of the fish but it should take about 20–30 minutes. Turn the fish once during cooking. Serve immediately.

Honey marinades

Simple honey marinades of the type used in this recipe are useful for pepping up all sorts of grills – from the humble sausage to grander gammon and turkey. Add fresh herbs of your choice and garlic too, if you like.

Gooseberry-stuffed Mackerel

The mixture of tart gooseberries with sweet honey forms a stuffing which perfectly complements the rich fish. Serve with boiled or creamed potatoes and a salad.Serves 4

Metric		Imperial
8 small *or* 4 large	mackerel, cleaned	8 small *or* 4 large
1	small onion	1
50 g	butter	2 oz
275 g	gooseberries, topped and tailed	10 oz
2 teaspoons	dried tarragon	2 teaspoons
	salt and freshly ground black pepper	
2 tablespoons	set honey	2 tablespoons
1	medium slice bread, crumbled	1

Cut the heads off the fish and open out the body.

To remove the bones from the fish, turn the flesh side down on a board and run your thumb down the backbone, pressing firmly. Turn the fish over and remove the bones – they should lift off easily in one complete section.

Finely chop the onion. Melt half the butter in a small saucepan, add the onion and cook for a few minutes until it is soft but not browned. Stir in the gooseberries, tarragon and seasoning. Continue to cook, stirring frequently over gentle heat, for about 5 minutes. Stir in the honey and remove the pan from the heat. Mix in the breadcrumbs, taste and adjust the seasoning if necessary.

Using your fingers, press a little stuffing into each fish. Fold the fish over to enclose the stuffing and lay close together in an ovenproof dish. Spoon any extra filling in between the fish in the dish. Dot with the remaining butter, cover the dish with foil and bake in a moderate oven (180 C, 350 F, gas 4) for about 45 minutes or until the fish is cooked through.

Fish Croquettes with Caper Sauce

You can serve this caper sauce with any poached or grilled fish fillets or steaks. These croquettes can also be served as a starter before a light main course. Serves 4

Metric		Imperial
350 g	potatoes	12 oz
450 g	white fish fillets	1 lb
	salt and freshly ground black pepper	
	flour to dust	
1	egg, beaten	1
100 g	dry breadcrumbs	4 oz
	oil for deep frying	
	Caper sauce	
2	egg yolks	2
5 teaspoons	cider vinegar	5 teaspoons
75 g	butter	3 oz
2 tablespoons	clear honey	2 tablespoons
2 tablespoons	chopped capers	2 tablespoons
	Garnish	
	sprigs of parsley	

Peel and cube the potatoes, then cook them in boiling salted water until tender. Drain and mash until smooth. Skin the fish (see page 19) then poach it in a little water or milk for 15–20 minutes. Drain, then flake and mash it, removing any remaining skin and bones. Mix the fish into the potatoes with plenty of seasoning. Shape into eight croquettes and dust each with a little flour. Dip these first in the beaten egg and then in the breadcrumbs to form an even coating.

Heat the oil for deep frying to 180 C / 350 F and cook the croquettes until golden brown and crisp. Drain on absorbent kitchen paper and keep hot while you make the sauce.

Whisk the egg yolks with the cider vinegar in a small bowl. Melt the butter with the honey, then gradually pour this over the yolks, whisking continuously. Stand the bowl over a saucepan of hot, not boiling, water and continue to whisk the sauce for about 5 minutes or until it has thickened slightly. Stir in the capers and season to taste. Do not allow the water to boil or the sauce will curdle.

Arrange the croquettes on a serving dish and pour over the sauce. Serve at once, garnished with the parsley.

Cod with Caraway Cucumber Sauce

This slightly unusual combination of flavours does, in fact, taste quite delicious. Sautéed or boiled potatoes are best to serve with this dish, and keep the other vegetables simple – cooked French beans, peas or broccoli. Serves 4

Metric		Imperial
675 g	cod fillet	1½ lb
1	onion	1
½	cucumber	½
1–2 tablespoons	flour	1–2 tablespoons
	salt and freshly ground black pepper	
50 g *or*	butter	2 oz *or*
2 tablespoons	oil	2 tablespoons
1 tablespoon	caraway seeds	1 tablespoon
300 ml	dry white wine	½ pint
2 tablespoons	clear honey	2 tablespoons
	Garnish	
1	lemon, cut into 8 wedges	1

Skin the fish (see page 19) and cut it into large chunks. halve and slice the onion, peel and dice the cucumber. Sprinkle the flour over the fish and season it generously.

Melt the butter or heat the oil in a fairly deep frying pan. Add the fish and cook, turning once or twice, until browned all over. Remove from the pan. Add the onion, cucumber and caraway to the fat remaining in the pan. Cook until the onion is soft but not browned. Pour in the wine and honey and bring to the boil. Return the fish to the pan, cover and simmer gently for 20 minutes.

Taste and adjust the seasoning before serving garnished with lemon wedges.

Beef with Chestnuts

Honey can be used to enrich savoury meat casseroles. Here, the combination of honey with bitter stout makes a rich and satisfying sauce. I have used a whole piece of stewing beef to make an interesting change, but you can use cut meat if you prefer. Serves 4–6

Metric		Imperial
1.25–1.5 kg	stewing steak, in one piece	2½–3 lb
2 tablespoons	flour	2 tablespoons
	salt and freshly ground black pepper	
	dripping or oil for shallow frying	
350 g	pickling onions	12 oz
2	bay leaves	2
4 tablespoons	set honey	4 tablespoons
600 ml	stout	1 pint
600 ml	beef stock	1 pint
100 g	dried chestnuts	4 oz

Tie the meat into a neat shape. Mix the flour with plenty of seasoning and coat the meat in it. Heat the dripping or oil in a frying pan, then add the meat and brown on all sides. Transfer the joint to a deep ovenproof casserole.

Add the onions and bay leaves to the fat left in the pan and cook until the onions are lightly browned. Transfer to the casserole. Stir the honey and stout into the juices left in the frying pan, heat to boiling point, then pour over the meat. Add the stock to the casserole and finally stir in the chestnuts.

Cover and cook in a moderate oven (160 C, 325 F, gas 3) for about 4 hours, or until the meat is tender. Turn the meat once or twice during cooking. Carefully remove the string and slice the meat to serve. Accompany with baked or roast potatoes and simple boiled vegetables.

Honey casseroles

Honey can be used to enrich various meat casseroles – particularly those made from pork or beef, and cooked in wine, cider or beer. Add the honey at the beginning of the cooking time and taste the sauce carefully to make sure that it is rich but not too sweet. About 2–3 tablespoons honey in a casserole to serve four should be sufficient.

Beef Patties with Orange Pepper Sauce

You can also serve these hamburgers in sesame buns for a light lunch or supper. Minced pork or lamb can be used instead of the beef.

Serves 4

Metric		Imperial
675 g	minced beef or steak	1½ lb
	salt and freshly ground black pepper	
	Orange pepper sauce	
1	onion	1
1	red or green pepper	1
2	oranges	2
25 g	butter	1 oz
1 tablespoon	flour	1 tablespoon
150 ml	beef stock	¼ pint
2 tablespoons	clear honey	2 tablespoons
	few sprigs of thyme	
	To serve	
	½ Chinese cabbage, shredded	

Mix the beef with plenty of seasoning then shape into four patties. Knead each portion of meat thoroughly into a ball first so that the patties will bind together well.

For the sauce, thinly slice the onion. Remove and discard the stalk, core and seeds from the pepper, then slice the shell into rings. Grate the rind from one of the oranges and squeeze the juice from both. Melt the butter in a saucepan, add the onion, pepper and seasoning. Cook until the onion is soft but not browned. Stir in the flour, then gradually add the orange rind, juice and stock. Stir in the honey and add the sprigs of thyme. Heat slowly to boiling point, then reduce the heat so that the sauce simmers gently as you cook the meat patties.

Place the patties under a hot grill and cook, turning once, until they are done to your taste. Allow about 3 minutes on each side for burgers rare in the middle, 4–5 minutes if you like them just a little pink, and about 7–8 minutes if you prefer the meat cooked right through.

Arrange the Chinese cabbage on a serving platter and lay the meat patties on top. Pour over the sauce and serve immediately.

Fresh Fruit and Nut Salad (page 87)
and Sausage and Bacon Rolls (page 23)

Chilli Pancakes

(Illustrated on page 52)
*Honey is such a versatile ingredient; in this recipe it is used to enrich
a traditional combination of meat, spices and beans. Serve these
pancakes with a salad. Serves 4*

Metric		Imperial
1	red pepper	1
1	large onion	1
1 tablespoon	oil	1 tablespoon
450 g	minced beef	1 lb
	salt and freshly ground black pepper	
1–2 tablespoons	chilli powder	1–2 tablespoons
2 tablespoons	clear honey	2 tablespoons
2 tablespoons	tomato purée	2 tablespoons
1 tablespoon	lemon juice	1 tablespoon
1	396-g/14-oz can tomatoes	1
150 ml	dry red wine	$\frac{1}{4}$ pint
double quantity	pancake batter (page 20)	double quantity
	oil for frying	
1	432-g/15¼-oz can red kidney beans	1

Remove and discard the stalk, core and seeds from the pepper. Finely chop
the pepper and onion. Heat the oil in a heavy-based saucepan or
flameproof casserole. Add the onion and pepper and cook until the onion
is soft but not browned. Add the beef, seasoning and chilli powder, then
continue to cook, stirring the meat frequently, until well browned. Stir in
the honey, tomato purée, lemon juice, tomatoes and wine. Bring to the
boil, cover and simmer gently for 40 minutes.

Meanwhile, make the pancake batter as described on page 20. Heat a
little oil in a frying pan and add enough batter to just cover the base of the
pan. Cook the pancake until golden brown on the underside, then turn
over and brown the second side. Repeat until all the batter is used, layering
the cooked pancakes with absorbent kitchen paper to prevent them
sticking together. This quantity of batter should make eight to ten large
pancakes. Keep warm in the oven until the filling is ready.

About 5 minutes before the end of the cooking time, add the beans to the
meat. Continue to cook gently; by the end of the cooking time the liquid
should have reduced to leave the meat and beans moist, not wet.

Fill the pancakes with the meat mixture, roll them over and serve
immediately.

Herb and Honey Chicken Pieces (page 55)

Pork Meatloaf

(Illustrated on page 85)
Serve this meatloaf hot with moist vegetable dishes such as cauliflower
cheese and braised celery, or cold with a crisp fresh salad. Serves 4–6

Metric		Imperial
1	large onion	1
50 g	button mushrooms	2 oz
225 g	smoked streaky bacon	8 oz
450 g	minced pork	1 lb
50 g	fresh breadcrumbs	2 oz
	salt and freshly ground black pepper	
2 tablespoons	chopped mixed fresh herbs	2 tablespoons
	grated rind of 1 orange	
1	egg	1
3 tablespoons	clear honey	3 tablespoons
	dash of Worcestershire sauce	

Finely chop the onion and mushrooms. Cut off and discard the rinds from
the bacon, then chop it finely. Mix these prepared ingredients into the
minced pork with the breadcrumbs and plenty of seasoning. Add the
herbs, orange rind, egg and honey. Mix thoroughly, adding a dash of
Worcestershire sauce.

Turn the meat mixture into a greased 450-g/1-lb loaf tin, pressing it
down well. Cover closely with a piece of greased cooking foil and stand the
tin in a bain marie – a roasting tin almost full of boiling water. Cook in a
moderate oven (160 C, 325 F, gas 3) for 1½ hours. Remove from the oven
and turn out if the meatloaf is to be served hot, or allow the meatloaf to
cool in the tin if it is to be served cold.

Spiced Pork with Apple Yogurt Sauce

Serve these chops with plain boiled rice, crisp poppadums and a small bowl of diced cucumber sprinkled with chilli powder. Serves 4

Metric		Imperial
4	pork chops	4
3	cardamom pods	3
4 tablespoons	grated fresh root ginger	4 tablespoons
3	cloves garlic, crushed	3
2 teaspoons	ground coriander	2 teaspoons
2 tablespoons	oil	2 tablespoons
1 teaspoon	white wine vinegar	1 teaspoon
1 tablespoon	clear honey	1 tablespoon
	salt and freshly ground black pepper	
	Sauce	
450 g	cooking apples	1 lb
3 tablespoons	clear honey	3 tablespoons
150 ml	natural yogurt	$\frac{1}{4}$ pint
4	spring onions, chopped	4
	Garnish	
1	dessert apple, cored and sliced	1

Trim any excess fat off the chops and place them in a shallow dish. Split the cardamom pods and remove the seeds. Mix with the ginger, garlic, coriander, oil and vinegar. Stir in the honey and seasoning, then spread this mixture over both sides of the chops. Cover and allow to stand for at least 1 hour. The longer the chops are left to marinate, the better the dish will taste – so if possible leave them in the refrigerator overnight.

To make the sauce, peel, core and thickly slice the cooking apples. Place in a saucepan with the honey and cook gently until the fruit is soft but not mushy. Meanwhile, cook the chops under a hot grill for about 30 minutes, turning them once and basting frequently until they are cooked through.

To finish the sauce, stir in the yogurt and spring onions and heat very gently for a few minutes to warm the yogurt. Do not overheat the sauce or the yogurt will curdle and look unappetising. To serve, arrange the chops on a serving dish and spoon any of the marinade over them. Garnish with slices of apple. Pour the sauce into a warmed sauceboat or jug and serve with the chops.

Pork Stir-fry

With the increased interest in Chinese food and cooking, it is now possible to buy specialist ingredients in many supermarkets. However, if you cannot find dried mushrooms, substitute four large open mushrooms. Serve the stir-fry with steamed or boiled rice and a dish of crisp-fried Chinese noodles. Serves 4

Metric		Imperial
350 g	lean boneless pork	12 oz
2	dried Chinese mushrooms	2
1	227-g/8-oz can water chestnuts	1
1	425-g/15-oz can whole baby sweet corn in brine	1
2 tablespoons	clear honey	2 tablespoons
3 tablespoons	light soy sauce	3 tablespoons
4 tablespoons	water	4 tablespoons
1 tablespoon	vinegar	1 tablespoon
2 tablespoons	light sesame oil or corn oil	2 tablespoons
2 teaspoons	cornflour	2 teaspoons
	Garnish	
	a few spring onion curls (see below)	

Cut the pork into very fine strips. Place the dried mushrooms in a small bowl and cover with hot water. Leave to stand for 15 minutes or until they are soft enough to cut. Meanwhile, drain and slice the water chestnuts and drain the sweet corn. Mix the honey with the soy sauce, water and vinegar.

Heat the oil in a heavy-based frying pan or wok. If you are using sesame oil take care not to overheat it or it will taste very bitter. Add the pork, mushrooms and water chestnuts to the pan and cook quickly, turning and tossing the food all the time. Sprinkle the cornflour into the pan and stir into the ingredients. Gradually pour in the liquid mixture and cook, stirring continuously, until it boils.

Stir in the sweet corn and continue to cook for a few minutes. Serve immediately, garnished with the spring onion curls.

Spring onion curls

Wash and trim a small bunch of spring onions, leaving plenty of the green part. Snip into the green part of the onion, cutting down as far as possible to make thin green strips, all attached at the base. Place these in a bowl of iced water, or place them in a bowl of water in the refrigerator, and leave to stand for at least 30 minutes. The longer the onions soak the more they will curl – you can cheerfully leave them overnight if you like.

Pork Stroganoff

This dish is very quick to prepare and is best served with plain boiled rice or pasta and a green salad. The honey enriches and slightly sweetens the stroganoff – a pleasant contrast to the soured cream. You can also make a beef stroganoff from this recipe – simply substitute frying steak for the pork. Serves 4

Metric		Imperial
675 g	lean boneless pork	1½ lb
2 teaspoons	paprika	2 teaspoons
2 teaspoons	flour	2 teaspoons
	salt and freshly ground black pepper	
100 g	button mushrooms	4 oz
25 g	butter	1 oz
2 tablespoons	clear honey	2 tablespoons
100 ml	dry red wine	4 fl oz
150 ml	soured cream	¼ pint
	a little chopped parsley	

Cut the pork into thin strips and place in a bowl. Add the paprika, flour and plenty of seasoning, then toss well to coat the meat. Finely slice the mushrooms.

Melt the butter in a frying pan, add the pork and cook quickly, turning the meat frequently, until evenly browned. Stir in the honey and wine and bring to the boil, then simmer for about 5 minutes. Stir in the soured cream and heat through without allowing the mixture to boil. Serve immediately, topped with a little chopped parsley.

Braised Pork Cutlets

(Illustrated on page 51)
*Honey enhances the flavour of pork, as shown in this dish – a rich
casserole which can be served with just a simple salad and some
bread, as the vegetables are already cooked with the meat. Serves 4*

Metric		Imperial
8	pork cutlets or small sparerib chops	8
1	green pepper	1
1	large onion	1
1 kg	new potatoes	2 lb
2 tablespoons	oil	2 tablespoons
	salt and freshly ground black pepper	
2	cloves garlic, crushed	2
2 tablespoons	flour	2 tablespoons
1	396-g/14-oz can tomatoes	1
450 ml	dry red wine	$\frac{3}{4}$ pint
3 tablespoons	tomato purée	3 tablespoons
3 tablespoons	clear honey	3 tablespoons
3	sprigs of rosemary	3

Trim the pork of any excess fat. Remove and discard the stalk, core and
seeds from the pepper, then cut it into slices. Chop the onion and slice the
new potatoes, or cut them in half if they are small.

Heat the oil in a large, fairly deep frying pan, heavy-based saucepan or
skillet. Add the pork and cook, turning once, until browned on both sides.
Remove from the pan and set aside. Add the potatoes to the fat remaining
in the pan and cook until lightly browned all over. Add the onion and
pepper and continue to cook, stirring, until the onion is soft but not
browned. Add seasoning to taste, the garlic and flour. Continue to cook,
stirring the flour into the other ingredients, for a few minutes. Pour the
tomatoes and wine into the pan, stir in the tomato purée and honey and
bring slowly to the boil. Meanwhile, chop the spiky leaves from the
rosemary and stir them into the sauce. Return the chops to the pan and
simmer gently, covered, for about 40 minutes, or until the chops and
potatoes are thoroughly cooked.

Taste and adjust the seasoning, then transfer to a warmed dish and serve
immediately.

Lamb and Aubergine Kebabs

Kebabs are easy to prepare, good to eat and yet look so impressive when neatly served. For a change, why not try serving this dish on a bed of cooked chick peas flavoured with chopped chives? Add two or three tomatoes, peeled and chopped, to give a colourful arrangement.
Serves 4

Metric		Imperial
450 g	lean boneless lamb	1 lb
2	aubergines	2
	salt and freshly ground black pepper	
100 g	button mushrooms	4 oz
	Marinade	
4 tablespoons	clear honey	4 tablespoons
4 tablespoons	natural yogurt	4 tablespoons
2	cloves garlic, crushed	2
2 teaspoons	dried oregano	2 teaspoons

Cut the lamb into neat cubes. Cut the stalk ends off the aubergines, then cut into cubes. Place in a colander or sieve over a bowl and sprinkle with a little salt. Remove the stalks from the mushrooms – reserve these for use in a casserole, pie or omelette.

Mix the ingredients for the marinade together, season and pour over the meat. Set aside for several hours. When the meat has marinated, rinse and dry the pieces of aubergine. Thread the meat, aubergine and mushrooms on to eight metal skewers. Cook under a hot grill, turning and basting with the marinade until the meat is cooked – this will take about 30 minutes. Serve immediately.

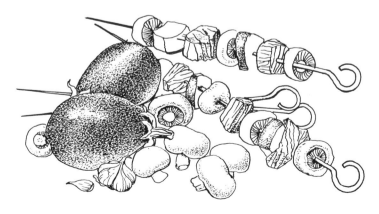

Apricot-stuffed Lamb

Stuffed joints of meat are moist to serve and offer a superior flavour. In addition, they are easier to carve and tend to go further than meat served on the bone. If you don't have a local butcher, ask if you can have a joint boned in your local supermarket. If the meat is butchered on the premises you may well find that someone is quite happy to remove the bone for you. If you have to tackle the task yourself, the advice given opposite may be of some help. Serves 6

Metric		Imperial
2-kg	shoulder of lamb, boned	4½-lb
1	clove garlic, peeled and halved	1
	salt and freshly ground black pepper	
225 g	dried apricots	8 oz
2	stalks celery	2
4 tablespoons	set honey	4 tablespoons
1 teaspoon	dried marjoram	1 teaspoon
2	sprigs of rosemary	2
2	medium slices bread	2
4 tablespoons	milk	4 tablespoons
4 tablespoons	fresh orange juice	4 tablespoons
1 tablespoon	flour	1 tablespoon
450 ml	chicken or vegetable stock or dry red wine	¾ pint

Trim any small lumps of fat off the meat and rub the garlic clove inside the cavity left by the bone. Sprinkle a little salt over the outside of the joint and set it aside while you prepare the stuffing.

Roughly chop the apricots and slice the celery, then mix these ingredients with 3 tablespoons of the honey and the marjoram. Chop the spiky leaves from the rosemary and add to the stuffing. Cut the minimum of crust off the bread, break up the slices and place in a bowl. Sprinkle over the milk and set aside for 2 minutes. Break up the soaked bread and mix it into the stuffing. Stir to combine the ingredients and add a little seasoning.

Using a small spoon and your fingers, press the stuffing into the cavity in the lamb. With a trussing needle or the largest darning needle you can find, sew up the joint to completely enclose the stuffing in a neat parcel. Place the lamb in a roasting tin.

Mix the remaining honey with the orange juice and brush a little over the lamb. Roast the joint in a moderately hot oven (200 C, 400 F, gas 6) for 15 minutes, then reduce the temperature to moderate (180 C, 350 F, gas 4) and cook for a further 1½–1¾ hours. During cooking baste the joint frequently with fat from the roasting tin and brush with a little more honey glaze.

Remove the meat from the tin and keep it hot while you prepare a gravy from the juices. Pour off most of the fat, leaving all the juices. Add the flour to the pan and cook over medium heat, stirring continuously, for a few minutes. Gradually stir in the stock or wine and bring to the boil. Continue to simmer the sauce for about 3 minutes, stirring the sauce and scraping all the juices from the pan. Serve to accompany the joint.

Variations

Apple-stuffed Lamb Peel, core and roughly chop 450 g/1 lb cooking apples. Substitute these for the dried apricots in the above recipe and use 1 tablespoon chopped fresh mint instead of the marjoram and rosemary.

Lamb with Mushrooms and Olives Substitute 50 g/2 oz cooked long-grain rice for the apricots in the above recipe. Add 100 g/4 oz sliced button mushrooms and 100 g/4 oz sliced stuffed green olives to the stuffing.

Boning meat

Before you start make sure that you have a sharp, pointed knife to hand; lock the family out of the kitchen and don't rush the job. Work slowly and carefully, cutting down the bone and pointing the knife in towards it. Ease and scrape the meat off the bone until you reach the other end when you can remove the bone completely. Don't be afraid of using your hands to push aside the meat as you cut it from the bone, or to feel for the direction in which the bone is lying.

Tie the meat into a neat shape if you are not going to stuff it. Brushed inside and out with a little clear honey and seasoned lightly, the roast joint will be delicious to eat and easy to carve.

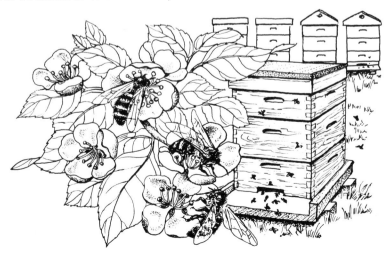

Marinated Breast of Lamb

Breast of lamb is inexpensive and well flavoured but it can be rather fatty, so a slightly sweetened, spicy glaze brings out the very best in this cut of meat. Serve with plain boiled rice and a bowl of chopped cucumber and natural yogurt. Serves 4

Metric		Imperial
1	breast of lamb, boned	1
3 tablespoons	set honey	3 tablespoons
2	cloves garlic, crushed	2
2 tablespoons	grated fresh root ginger	2 tablespoons
	grated rind and juice of 1 lemon	
2 tablespoons	chopped fresh coriander (optional)	2 tablespoons
	salt and freshly ground black pepper	
	Garnish	
1	lemon, cut into wedges	1
1	bunch of spring onions, trimmed and made into curls (page 38)	1

Trim any excess fat from the lamb and lay it skin side down on a board. Mix the honey with the garlic, ginger, lemon rind and juice. Stir in the coriander (if used) and plenty of seasoning. Spread half this mixture over the lamb and fold it in half. Spread half the remaining paste on top of the folded lamb, then transfer it to a shallow dish, placing the pasted side down. Spread the remaining paste on top. Cover and leave to marinate overnight, or for up to three days if possible.

Roast the lamb, laid flat in a roasting tin, in a moderate oven (180 C, 350 F, gas 4) for about 1¼–1½ hours. Baste and turn the lamb frequently during cooking, then serve cut into strips and garnished with the lemon wedges and spring onions.

Tarragon Meatballs

There are times when we all despair at the thought of having to concoct something wonderful from the same old pound of mince. Well, here is a recipe which uses minced lamb – many supermarkets now sell it, or your butcher will usually oblige by mincing up a cheaper cut of lamb for you. You can, of course, make these meatballs from minced beef, but they really are rather special made from lamb.
Serves 4

Metric		Imperial
450 g	minced lamb	1 lb
1	medium slice bread, crumbled	1
1	egg, beaten	1
	salt and freshly ground black pepper	
1	onion	1
2	stalks celery (optional)	2
225 g	carrots	8 oz
25 g *or*	butter	1 oz *or*
2 tablespoons	oil	2 tablespoons
1 tablespoon	dried tarragon	1 tablespoon
2 tablespoons	clear honey	2 tablespoons
1 tablespoon	cider vinegar	1 tablespoon
300 ml	dry cider	½ pint

Mix the meat with the bread, egg and plenty of seasoning. Make sure all the ingredients are thoroughly combined, then take spoonfuls of the mixture and knead them into meatballs about the size of an egg.

Chop the onion, slice the celery, if used, and slice the carrots. Set aside while you fry the meatballs. Melt the butter or heat the oil in a fairly deep frying pan or skillet. Add the meatballs and fry them, turning occasionally, until browned on all sides. Remove from the pan. Add the prepared vegetables to the fat remaining in the pan and cook until soft but not browned. Stir the vegetables occasionally to prevent them sticking to the pan.

Add the tarragon and pour in the honey, cider vinegar and cider. Bring to the boil, stirring, then return the meatballs to the pan and continue to cook very gently for about 30 minutes, turning the meatballs once to make sure that they are cooked through.

Transfer to a serving dish and accompany with boiled white or brown rice or buttered pasta.

Honey-glazed Ham

When you consider that a joint of gammon is a solid piece of meat with no bone to discard and little or no fat to waste, it does not appear as extravagant a buy as you may at first think. And honey-glazed ham is delicious – hot with boiled or creamed potatoes and almost any vegetable, or cold with salads, bread and pickles. Why not treat the family to a special summer picnic with an impressive gammon centrepiece? Serves 4

Metric		Imperial
1.5-kg	corner or middle gammon joint	3-lb
	cloves	
	grated rind and juice of 1 orange	
3 tablespoons	clear honey	3 tablespoons

Place the gammon in a large saucepan and cover with cold water. Bring slowly to the boil, then discard the water and rinse the joint. Cover with fresh cold water and bring to the boil. Reduce the heat and cover the pan, then simmer very gently for an hour.

Drain the gammon, reserving the stock for making soup if you like. Carefully cut the skin off the joint and score the fat in a diamond pattern. Place the meat in a small roasting tin and stud the top with cloves.

Mix the orange rind and juice with the honey and pour this over the joint, brushing the liquid over the sides as you do so. Bake in a moderately hot oven (200 C, 400 F, gas 6) for about 30–40 minutes, or until the fat is golden brown. Baste the gammon frequently during cooking. Serve hot or cold – if you are serving the joint cold, continue to baste it with the glaze as it cools.

Variations

Honey and Apple Ham Boil the joint as above. Omit the orange rind and juice from the glaze but add 150 ml/¼ pint apple juice to the honey. Peel and core 4 medium cooking apples and place them in the roasting tin with the studded ham. Pour the glaze over the gammon and the apples. Cook as above. Serve the gammon hot with the apples.

Nutty Honey Ham Boil the joint as above and prepare the orange and honey glaze. Do not stud the gammon with cloves but mix 50 g/2 oz finely chopped salted peanuts into the glaze. Pour this over the meat, pressing the nuts into the fat with the back of a metal spoon. Bake as above and serve hot or cold.

Gammon Steaks en Croûte

Gammon steaks are expensive but here is a recipe which takes just two steaks to serve four people. The result is quite filling and certainly does not appear to be skimpy. Served with a crisp bean sprout salad or a simple green salad and small new potatoes, this recipe would be ideal for a special supper treat. Serves 4

Metric		Imperial
2	thick gammon steaks	2
1	red or green pepper	1
1	227-g/8-oz can pineapple rings in natural juice	1
1	small onion	1
2 tablespoons	clear honey	2 tablespoons
1	clove garlic, crushed	1
	salt and freshly ground black pepper	
1	370-g/13-oz packet frozen puff pastry, thawed	1
	beaten egg to glaze	

Trim the rind off the gammon steaks and cut them in half. Cut the pepper in half, remove and discard the seeds, core and stalk, then chop the flesh. Drain the juice from the pineapple and reserve it for another use, or pour it into a glass and drink up as you prepare the recipe! Chop the pineapple rings and the onion, then mix both with the pepper. Stir in the honey and garlic and add seasoning to taste. Set aside.

Cut the pastry into four and roll out each portion to give an oblong large enough to enclose a piece of the gammon. Place a half gammon steak on each piece of pastry and top with the pineapple and pepper mixture. Working fairly quickly, brush the edges of the pastry with a little water, then fold them up around the gammon and seal together over the filling. Try to keep all the juices from the filling within the pastry case.

Transfer the parcels to a dampened baking tray and brush with a little beaten egg. Bake in a hot oven (230 C, 450 F, gas 8) for 20 minutes, then reduce to moderately hot (200 C, 400 F, gas 6) for a further 15 minutes. Serve immediately.

Sausage and Apple Pie

A layer of chopped apples with honey and oregano livens up a simple sausagemeat pie. Serve the pie hot with creamed or baked potatoes and buttered green vegetables, or serve it cold with a salad. Serves 6

Metric		Imperial
	Wholemeal pastry	
225 g	wholemeal flour	8 oz
	pinch of salt	
175 g	margarine	6 oz
4 tablespoons	water	4 tablespoons
	beaten egg to glaze	
	Filling	
1	large onion	1
50 g	smoked streaky bacon	2 oz
450 g	pork sausagemeat	1 lb
	dash of Worcestershire sauce	
	salt and freshly ground black pepper	
3	small cooking apples	3
2 teaspoons	dried oregano	2 teaspoons
2 tablespoons	clear honey	2 tablespoons

Place the flour in a bowl with the salt. Add the margarine, cut into small pieces, and rub it in until the mixture resembles fine breadcrumbs. Sprinkle the water over and mix together lightly to form a dough. Roll out two-thirds of this pastry and use to line a 23-cm/9-in pie plate.

To prepare the filling, first finely chop the onion. Trim the rinds off the bacon, then chop it finely. Mix the onion and bacon into the sausagemeat, seasoning with the Worcestershire sauce, salt and pepper. Peel, core and chop the apples, then mix them with the oregano and honey.

Spread half the sausagemeat mixture in the pie and top with the apple mixture, pressing it down well into the meat. Spread the remaining sausagemeat on top. Roll out the remaining pastry into a circle large enough to cover the pie. Dampen the edges of the pastry base with a little water, then carefully lift the pastry lid over the filling.

Press the pastry together to seal the edges, then trim and flute them between your fingers. Use any trimmings to decorate the top of the pie and cut two small slits in the top. Brush with beaten egg and bake in a moderately hot oven (200 F, 400 F, gas 6) for 30 minutes. Reduce the oven temperature to moderate (180 C, 350 F, gas 4) and cook for a further 40–45 minutes.

Pastry edges

There are several simple techniques which you can use to decorate the edges of a savoury pie. They can be fluted by gently pinching the pastry between your finger and thumb at equal intervals around the pie. Alternatively, to make a scalloped border, press the edges outwards with your index finger and pull in the pastry with the blunt edge of a knife. Move around the pie, pressing out the pastry and pulling in the edges at equal intervals to make neat scallops.

Smoked Sausage with Chick Peas

Here is a quick, economical and tasty dish which can be served with just wholemeal or granary bread and a green salad. Serves 4

Metric		Imperial
1 tablespoon	mustard with chives	1 tablespoon
2 tablespoons	clear honey	2 tablespoons
1	240-g/8-oz smoked Dutch sausage	1
1	onion	1
100 g	white cabbage	4 oz
25 g or	butter	1 oz or
1 tablespoon	oil	1 tablespoon
1	clove garlic, crushed	1
1	400-g/14-oz can chick peas, drained	1
1	396-g/14-oz can tomatoes	1
	salt and freshly ground black pepper	

Mix the mustard with the honey and spread this mixture over the sausage. Set aside.

Chop the onion and finely shred the cabbage. Melt the butter or heat the oil in a frying pan. Add the onion and garlic and cook until the onion is soft but not browned. Add the cabbage and cook for a further 2–3 minutes before stirring in the chick peas, tomatoes and seasoning to taste. Allow this mixture to simmer gently while you cook the sausage.

Lay the sausage on a foil-lined grill pan and cook under a hot grill for about 10 minutes, turning once to brown both sides. Slice the cooked sausage and serve it on top of the chick pea mixture. Eat at once.

Cider-glazed Chicken

This chicken tastes excellent eaten either hot or served cold with salads. Serve the hot chicken in its glaze, with buttered noodles and a crisp mixed salad. If you prefer to serve the dish cold, remove the chicken from the oven and baste it frequently with the glaze until it is completely cold. Lightly chill the bird and serve it garnished with salad ingredients. Serves 4

Metric		Imperial
1	small onion, halved	1
1.5-kg	oven-ready chicken	3-lb
3 tablespoons	clear honey	3 tablespoons
1	clove garlic, crushed	1
2 teaspoons	mustard powder	2 teaspoons
	salt and freshly ground black pepper	
3	bay leaves	3
450 ml	dry cider	$\frac{3}{4}$ pint

Place the onion halves inside the body cavity of the chicken, then sit it in an ovenproof casserole. Mix the honey with the garlic, mustard and plenty of seasoning. Spread this mixture over the chicken and place the bay leaves on top of the bird. Cook in a moderately hot oven (190 C, 375 F, gas 5) for 40 minutes.

Warm the cider, then carefully pour it over the chicken and continue to cook, uncovered, for a further 50–60 minutes. Baste the chicken frequently during cooking and cover it loosely with a little foil if it becomes too dark.

At the end of the cooking time, drain the liquid from the chicken and transfer it to a saucepan. Return the bird to the oven to keep hot while you reduce the sauce. To do this, bring the liquid to the boil, then cook, uncovered, until it is reduced by about three-quarters of its original quantity. The sauce should boil for about 10–15 minutes to make it thick enough.

Place the chicken on a serving dish and pour over the glaze. Serve immediately.

Braised Pork Cutlets (page 40)

Devilled Drumsticks

Serve these drumsticks either hot on a bed of cooked rice or cold with a rice salad. If you are planning to serve a light main course, one drumstick per person can also make a tasty appetiser. Serves 4

Metric		Imperial
1	small onion	1
1 teaspoon	ground ginger	1 teaspoon
1 teaspoon	paprika	1 teaspoon
2	cloves garlic, crushed	2
1 tablespoon	cider vinegar	1 tablespoon
2 tablespoons	clear honey	2 tablespoons
	dash of Worcestershire sauce	
	salt and freshly ground black pepper	
8	chicken drumsticks	8
	Garnish	
	a little chopped parsley	
1	small onion, sliced into rings	1

Grate the onion into a bowl, then add the ginger, paprika, garlic and vinegar. Stir in the honey and a dash of Worcestershire sauce, then season the mixture generously. Cut two or three diagonal slits into the drumsticks, then place in a shallow dish and spread the onion mixture over them. Set aside for several hours, preferably overnight. While the chicken is marinating, turn the pieces over once or twice to make sure they are completely covered with the sauce.

Cook the chicken under a hot grill, on a foil-lined grill pan. As they cook, baste the drumsticks frequently with the marinade and turn them several times. The cooking time will depend upon the size of the chicken pieces but it should be about 20–25 minutes. If the chicken is browning too quickly, reduce the heat from the grill. When cooked, the juices from the chicken will run clear with no sign of blood.

Arrange the drumsticks on a dish of cooked rice, if you like, then garnish with a little chopped parsley and onion rings. Serve two drumsticks to each person.

Apple Pancakes (page 76), Chilli Pancakes (page 35) and Seafood Pancakes (page 20)

Duck with Juniper

Here is a rich dish to cook on special occasions. Serve swirls of piped mashed potato, browned under the grill, and lightly cooked courgettes, braised chicory or fennel as accompaniments. Serves 4

Metric		Imperial
3 tablespoons	set honey	3 tablespoons
1	clove garlic, crushed	1
1 tablespoon	juniper berries, crushed	1 tablespoon
	salt and freshly ground black pepper	
1.5–1.7-kg	duck	3½–4-lb
2 tablespoons	flour	2 tablespoons
300 ml	full-bodied red wine	½ pint
	Garnish	
	watercress	

Mix the honey with the garlic, juniper and plenty of seasoning. Remove the giblets from the duck. Prick the skin all over with a fork and spread the honey mixture over the duck. Leave to marinate – overnight if possible, if not then for as many hours as you can spare.

Place the giblets in a small saucepan and cover them with cold water. Bring to the boil, cover and reduce the heat then simmer for about 1 hour. Cool, strain and reserve the stock.

Transfer the bird to a roasting tin and pour the marinade over. Roast the duck in a hot oven (220 C, 425 F, gas 7) for 10 minutes, then reduce the temperature to moderate (180 C, 350 F, gas 4) and cook for about 1¼ hours. Baste the duck frequently and check that it does not become too dark during cooking. If it is browning too quickly, place a piece of cooking foil loosely over the top.

Lift the duck out of the roasting tin and transfer to a warmed serving dish. Keep hot while you prepare the sauce. Pour off most of the fat from the roasting tin, leaving just the meat juices. Over low heat, add the flour to the pan and stir for about 2 minutes. Make up the reserved giblet stock to 300 ml/½ pint with water if necessary; don't worry if you have too much stock, you can reduce it later.

Gradually pour the stock and wine into the pan, stirring continuously to prevent lumps forming. Bring the sauce to the boil, then reduce the heat and simmer for 2–3 minutes. Taste and adjust the seasoning and continue cooking for a few minutes if the sauce is not concentrated enough for your taste.

Garnish the duck with a little watercress and serve the sauce in a warmed sauceboat.

Variations

Honey Orange Duck Omit the juniper berries and garlic from the marinade. Mix the honey with the grated rind and juice of 1 orange and continue as above. Peel and remove the segments from 2 oranges and add these to the sauce before serving the duck.

Plum Duck Omit the juniper berries from the marinade and add an extra clove of garlic. Cook the duck as above, adding 450 g/1 lb stoned plums to the sauce before you set it to simmer. Simmer until the plums are soft. Joint the cooked duck, if you like, and pour the sauce over it to serve.

Herb and Honey Chicken Pieces

(Illustrated on page 34)
In this simple recipe, the combination of herbs and honey imparts a delicious flavour to the chicken, at the same time sealing in the juices to keep the meat succulent and moist. Serves 4

Metric		Imperial
2 tablespoons	clear honey	2 tablespoons
8	chicken thighs or breasts, skinned	8
4 tablespoons	dried breadcrumbs	4 tablespoons
2 teaspoons	dried mixed herbs	2 teaspoons
	salt and freshly ground black pepper	
	pinch of cayenne	
	Garnish	
	lemon slices	
	sprigs of parsley	

Brush the honey over the chicken pieces. Mix the breadcrumbs and herbs on a plate. Add seasoning to taste and a little cayenne. Roll the chicken in the breadcrumb mixture, then place the pieces on a baking tray.

Bake in a moderately hot oven (190 C, 375 F, gas 5) for about 30 minutes, or until the chicken is golden brown and cooked through. Serve immediately, on a bed of cooked rice if you like, garnished with halved lemon slices and parsley.

Walnut and Apple Kebabs

Some nut dishes can be rather dry and monotonous – but not this one. Here is a lively combination of nuts, vegetables and fruit, carefully flavoured with honey and herbs. Serve the kebabs on a bed of cooked brown rice, cooked buckwheat or millet, and offer a salad tossed in a creamy dressing as an accompaniment. Serves 4

Metric		Imperial
225 g	walnut pieces	8 oz
1	large onion	1
2 tablespoons	olive oil	2 tablespoons
1 tablespoon	chopped parsley	1 tablespoon
1 tablespoon	chopped fresh lemon balm	1 tablespoon
2	sprigs of thyme	2
225 g	fresh brown breadcrumbs	8 oz
	salt and freshly ground black pepper	
4 tablespoons	clear honey	4 tablespoons
	dash of Worcestershire sauce	
2 teaspoons	mustard with chives	2 teaspoons
2	small cooking apples	2
2	small red peppers	2
24–32	small button mushrooms	24–32
	oil for brushing	

Grind the walnuts to a powder. Finely chop the onion. Heat the oil in a small frying pan, add the onion and cook until soft but not browned. Mix the nuts with the onion, parsley and lemon balm. Chop the thyme and add to the nut mixture. Add the breadcrumbs and seasoning to taste. Stir in the honey, Worcestershire sauce and mustard. Bind all the ingredients together and set aside.

Peel, quarter and core the apples, then cut each quarter into four pieces. Wrap each piece of apple in a portion of the nut mixture, kneading it around the apple to form smooth balls.

Remove and discard the stalks, cores and seeds from the peppers, then cut each into 16 pieces. Thread the apple and nut balls, pieces of pepper and the mushrooms on to eight metal skewers. Brush with a little oil and cook under a hot grill for about 5–7 minutes, turning once, until the peppers and mushrooms are lightly cooked and the nut mixture is browned. Brush with more oil as the kebabs cook. Serve immediately.

Lentil Patties with Cashew Sauce

Serve these savoury patties with baked potatoes, or buttered new potatoes sprinkled with a little lemon rind, and a salad – try a spinach salad, for example. Serves 4

Metric		Imperial
175 g	lentils	6 oz
450 ml	water	$\frac{3}{4}$ pint
1	large onion	1
4 tablespoons	wholewheat flour	4 tablespoons
2 tablespoons	chopped mixed fresh herbs	2 tablespoons
	salt and freshly ground black pepper	
	a little grated nutmeg	
	oil for shallow frying	
	Cashew sauce	
1	small red pepper	1
75 g	cashew nuts	3 oz
50 g *or*	butter	2 oz *or*
2 tablespoons	oil	2 tablespoons
	dash of soy sauce	
1 tablespoon	clear honey	1 tablespoon
2 tablespoons	natural yogurt	2 tablespoons

Rinse the lentils, then place them in a saucepan with the water. Bring to the boil, reduce the heat and cover the pan. Simmer until all the water has been absorbed but take care not to let the lentils burn. Remove the pan from the heat and allow to cool.

Chop the onion very finely, then mix it into the lentils with the flour and herbs. Add seasoning to taste and a little grated nutmeg. Shape the mixture into eight patties measuring about 10 cm/4 in. in diameter. You will find this easier if you work on a well-floured board or surface and keep your hands floured as you shape the mixture. Fry the patties fairly slowly in a shallow pan until they are golden brown on the underside. Turn them over and brown the second side.

Meanwhile, prepare the sauce. Remove and discard the stalk, core and seeds from the pepper. Finely chop the pepper shell and chop the cashew nuts. Melt the butter or heat the oil in a small saucepan, then add the nuts and pepper. Cook until the pepper is soft. Stir in the remaining ingredients and heat the sauce gently without boiling, or the yogurt will curdle.

Arrange the patties on a serving dish. Taste and season the sauce, then pour it over the patties. Serve immediately.

Aduki Beanpot

If you have never made a bean dish other than chilli con carne, then here is an excellent introductory recipe to present to your family or friends. Again, honey is used for its flavour and to enrich the dish: the nutty beans absorb its sweetness. Serve cooked brown rice and cooked cauliflower sprinkled with a mixture of grated cheese and walnuts as accompaniments. Serves 4

Metric		Imperial
225 g	aduki beans	8 oz
1	onion	1
2	stalks celery	2
1	large clove garlic	1
100 g	button mushrooms	4 oz
3 tablespoons	olive oil	3 tablespoons
	salt and freshly ground black pepper	
1	396-g/14-oz can tomatoes	1
3 tablespoons	clear honey	3 tablespoons
2 tablespoons	chopped mixed fresh herbs	2 tablespoons
	Garnish	
2	slices wholemeal bread	2
3 tablespoons	oil	3 tablespoons

Place the beans in a basin, cover with cold water and leave to soak overnight. Drain and rinse the beans, remove any that have not absorbed the water and transfer the remainder to a saucepan. Cover with plenty of cold water and bring to the boil. Reduce the heat, cover the pan and allow to simmer for 30–40 minutes until the beans are tender. Do not overcook the beans or they will become mushy. Drain and set aside.

At this stage you can prepare the croûtons to garnish the dish. Trim the crusts off the bread and cut the slices into neat cubes. Heat the oil in a frying pan, add the bread cubes and toss them in the oil, then cook, turning frequently, until crisp and browned all over. Drain on absorbent kitchen paper and set aside.

Chop the onion, slice the celery and chop the garlic. Slice the mushrooms and set aside. Heat the oil in a saucepan, add the onion, celery and garlic and cook until the onion is soft but not browned. Add seasoning to taste and stir in the mushrooms.

Pour in the tomatoes and honey, then add the herbs and cooked beans. Stir gently and heat slowly to boiling point. Reduce the heat so that the mixture cooks gently for a few minutes, allowing the flavours to mingle.

Sprinkle the croûtons over the beanpot, then serve straightaway.

Note: Aduki beans are small red beans, almost round in shape, with a nutty flavour. Red kidney beans, butter beans or chick peas can be substituted for aduki beans in the beanpot recipe but remember to allow a little extra cooking time if necessary.

Chick Peas with Mushrooms

Here, the delicate yet distinct flavour of honey complements the nutty flavour of the chick peas. Serve this dish with a fresh vegetable salad and some wholemeal or granary bread, or spoon the chick pea mixture over a bed of cooked brown rice mixed with toasted chopped almonds. For non-vegetarian meals it can also be served as an accompaniment to grilled meats or kebabs. Serves 2–4

Metric		Imperial
175 g	chick peas	6 oz
1	onion	1
175 g	mushrooms	6 oz
1 tablespoon	lemon juice	1 tablespoon
2 tablespoons	olive oil	2 tablespoons
1	clove garlic, crushed	1
	salt and freshly ground black pepper	
1 teaspoon	dried marjoram	1 teaspoon
2 tablespoons	clear honey	2 tablespoons
	Garnish	
	lemon slices or wedges	

Soak the chick peas overnight in cold water to cover. Drain off the water and discard any peas that have not absorbed the liquid or look black and discoloured. Place the remainder in a saucepan and cover with plenty of cold water. Bring to the boil, reduce the heat and cover the pan. Simmer for about 40–45 minutes or until the chick peas are tender. Drain off the water and set aside the peas.

Chop the onion and slice the mushrooms. Sprinkle the lemon juice over the mushrooms. Heat the oil in a saucepan, then add the onion, garlic and plenty of seasoning. Cook, stirring occasionally, until the onion is soft but not browned. Stir in the marjoram, chick peas and mushrooms. Continue to cook until the chick peas are heated through. Finally stir in the honey and cook for a minute then serve garnished with the lemon slices or wedges.

Vegetables and Salads

Fresh vegetables play an important part in a healthy diet and if you're trying to cut down on the calories then salads are a must.

Both raw and cooked, vegetables can be used as a main dish or to accompany other recipes. It is, however, a shame that vegetable dishes are often unimaginative and overcooked, just a boring necessity at every mealtime. With a little thought fresh foods of this sort can be used in recipes which make, not break, the meal, offering interesting textures and light fresh flavours.

Honey is an invaluable sweetening and flavouring agent for all types of salad dressings as well as light sauces. It is used with care in this chapter to give appeal to simple dishes, like Lemon Roast Potatoes and Braised Red Cabbage. The results are particularly lively and the dishes make an exciting change from boiled greens!

Honey-braised Red Cabbage

This dish makes an ideal accompaniment to grilled pork or lamb chops, sausages, both continental and English, as well as pies, meatloaves or hamburgers. Serves 4

Metric		Imperial
450 g	red cabbage	1 lb
1	large onion	1
1	stalk celery	1
2	medium cooking apples	2
2 tablespoons	oil	2 tablespoons
	salt and freshly ground black pepper	
3 tablespoons	clear honey	3 tablespoons
2 tablespoons	water	2 tablespoons
3 tablespoons	cider vinegar	3 tablespoons

Shred the cabbage, slice the onion and celery, peel, core and thickly slice the apples.

Heat the oil in a fairly deep frying pan or skillet, add the onion, cabbage and celery and season to taste. Cook, stirring, for 2–3 minutes, then stir in the honey and water and continue to cook until the mixture boils. Cover the pan, reduce the heat and simmer for 5–15 minutes, depending on how tender you want the cabbage. After 5 minutes the vegetables will still be very crunchy, after 15 minutes they will be cooked enough to give a very soft result at the end of the cooking time.

Add the apples and cider vinegar, stir them into the cabbage and cook, uncovered, over high heat until most of the liquid has evaporated to leave a moist glaze on the cabbage. Stir frequently as the mixture cooks to prevent it burning. Serve immediately.

Lemon Roast Potatoes

Serve these scrumptious potatoes with roast lamb or pork, casseroles or pies. Serves 4

Metric		Imperial
8	medium potatoes	8
	salt and freshly ground black pepper	
	grated rind and juice of 1 lemon	
2 tablespoons	clear honey	2 tablespoons
	dripping, butter or oil for cooking	

Cut the potatoes in half and cook them in lightly salted boiling water for 5 minutes. Drain and transfer to a roasting tin or ovenproof dish. Sprinkle over the lemon rind and juice and season with salt and pepper. Trickle the honey over the potatoes and dot them generously with dripping, butter or oil, or a mixture of butter and oil.

Roast in a moderately hot oven (200 C, 400 F, gas 6) for about 50–60 minutes, or until the potatoes are cooked through with a crisp, golden skin. Baste and turn the potatoes two or three times during cooking. Serve immediately.

Note: If you are cooking these at the same time as a roast joint, allow an extra 15 minutes in a moderate oven (180 C, 350 F, gas 4).

Flageolets

Serve this delicious bean dish as an accompaniment to roast or grilled lamb and lamb casseroles. It will, in fact, complement most meat casseroles, kebabs or grills. Serves 4

Metric		Imperial
225 g	flageolet beans	8 oz
1	onion	1
50 g	butter	2 oz
	salt and freshly ground black pepper	
2 tablespoons	clear honey	2 tablespoons

Soak the flageolets in cold water to cover for several hours or overnight. Drain and transfer the beans to a saucepan. Cover with plenty of cold water and bring to the boil. Cover the pan and reduce the heat, then simmer for about 40 minutes or until the flageolets are tender. Drain and set aside.

Halve and slice the onion. Melt the butter in a saucepan, add the onion and seasoning, then cook until soft but not browned. Stir in the honey and cooked beans. Heat through, tossing the beans in the sauce, and serve immediately.

Note: Flageolet beans are pale green in colour and oblong in shape. They are thin, quite small beans when dried and can also be purchased in cans. For quickness, the canned variety can be used in the above recipe.

Braised Celery with Carrots

This is a colourful vegetable which will moisten those meat or fish dishes with little or no sauce – grilled or fried foods and simple roasts, for example. Serves 4

Metric		Imperial
1	head celery	1
350 g	carrots	12 oz
1	onion	1
50 g	butter	2 oz
	salt and freshly ground black pepper	
200 ml	chicken stock	7 fl oz
2 tablespoons	clear honey	2 tablespoons
	dash of lemon juice	
	sprinkling of dill weed	
1 tablespoon	flour	1 tablespoon

Separate the celery into stalks, then cut each into two or three pieces. Halve or quarter the carrots lengthwise or leave whole if they are small. Thinly slice the onion.

Melt half the butter in a heavy-based saucepan or flameproof casserole. Add the onion and seasoning to taste, then cook until soft but not browned. Add the celery and carrots and cook, stirring, for a few minutes. Pour in the stock, honey and lemon juice. Sprinkle over the dill and heat slowly to boiling point. Reduce the heat and cover the pan, then simmer the vegetables very slowly for 30–40 minutes or until the celery is tender.

Cream the remaining butter with the flour, then add small pieces of this mixture to the sauce in the pan, stirring continuously over low heat. Bring to the boil, simmer for a minute to thicken, and serve.

Aubergines in Basil Sauce

Rich, sweet and sour is perhaps the best way to describe the sauce poured over the aubergines in this dish. The result is mouth-watering and gives an accompaniment which is excellent with grills and particularly lamb dishes. In fact, these aubergines are good enough to eat with just buttered pasta and a sprinkling of Parmesan cheese.
Serves 4

Metric		Imperial
2	large aubergines	2
	salt and freshly ground black pepper	
4 tablespoons	olive oil	4 tablespoons
1	onion	1
1	clove garlic, crushed	1
2 teaspoons	dried basil	2 teaspoons
2 tablespoons	cider vinegar	2 tablespoons
2 tablespoons	clear honey	2 tablespoons
2 tablespoons	tomato purée	2 tablespoons

Trim the stalks off the aubergines and cut them lengthwise into quarters. Place the pieces on a plate and sprinkle over a little salt. Leave to stand for about 20 minutes, then drain, rinse and dry.

Heat the oil in a shallow frying pan. Add the aubergine and fry on all sides until lightly browned and cooked through. Meanwhile, slice the onion and separate the slices into rings. Remove the cooked aubergine from the pan and transfer to a heated serving dish. Keep hot while you make the sauce.

Add the onion rings and garlic to the oil remaining in the pan. Add seasoning to taste and cook until lightly browned. Using a slotted spoon, remove the onion slices from the pan and arrange them on top of the aubergines. Stir the remaining ingredients into the oil and juices in the frying pan and heat to boiling point. Pour over the aubergines and serve.

Stuffed Courgettes

*The delicate flavour of courgettes is complemented by this stuffing
well-flavoured with bacon, honey and herbs. Serve these vegetables as
a starter with brown bread and butter, or with new potatoes and a
tomato salad for lunch or supper. Serves 4*

Metric		Imperial
4	courgettes	4
1	onion	1
3	rashers smoked streaky bacon	3
50 g	butter	2 oz
100 g	fresh breadcrumbs	4 oz
	salt and freshly ground black pepper	
	generous pinch each of dried thyme and marjoram	
1	egg	1
2 tablespoons	clear honey	2 tablespoons

Blanch the whole courgettes in boiling water for 3 minutes. Drain, cool and
reserve.

Meanwhile, finely chop the onion. Cut the rinds off the bacon and chop
it finely. Melt the butter in a small frying pan, add the onion and cook until
soft but not browned. Stir in the bacon and cook for a further 2 minutes.
Remove the pan from the heat and stir in the remaining ingredients to
make a soft stuffing.

Cut the courgettes in half lengthwise, Scoop out the middle and add this
to the stuffing, chopping it first if not soft enough to break up as you stir it
in. Using a teaspoon, fill the courgette shells with the stuffing and place
under the grill. Cook under medium heat until lightly browned on top.
Serve immediately.

Walnut-filled Fennel

Serve this dish for an interesting light main course. Alternatively, offer it as an accompaniment or an appetising starter. Serves 2–4

Metric		Imperial
4	large heads fennel	4
50 g	fresh breadcrumbs	2 oz
75 g	walnuts, chopped	3 oz
2 tablespoons	clear honey	2 tablespoons
1 tablespoon	chopped chives	1 tablespoon
1 tablespoon	milk	1 tablespoon
	salt and freshly ground black pepper	
50 g	butter	2 oz

Cut around the core of each fennel and up into the middle to remove a cone-shaped piece of vegetable. Check that there is a reasonably large cavity to fill with stuffing; if not, cut out a little more vegetable. Chop up most of the cut out fennel, discarding just the hard core.

Mix the remaining ingredients, apart from the butter, with the chopped fennel, and make sure that the mixture is well seasoned. Press this stuffing into the cavities left in the fennel and place in an ovenproof dish. Dot with the butter and cover closely with cooking foil. Bake in a moderate oven (180 C, 350 F, gas 4) for about 1½ hours, or until the fennel is tender. Serve.

Parma Chicory with Apricots

Delicate, delicious and rather expensive – a dish to be served as a first course or to accompany simple main dishes like grilled chicken breasts, veal escalopes and grilled steak. Serves 4

Metric		Imperial
4	heads chicory	4
	salt and freshly ground black pepper	
1	onion	1
25 g	butter	1 oz
100 g	dried apricots	4 oz
2 tablespoons	clear honey	2 tablespoons
300 ml	dry white wine	½ pint
4	slices Parma ham	4

Blanch the chicory in lightly salted boiling water for 2 minutes. Drain and set aside.

Finely chop the onion. Melt the butter in a flameproof casserole, add the onion and cook until soft but not browned. Roughly chop the apricots and add them to the onion, then stir in the honey and wine. Add seasoning to taste, and heat slowly to boiling point.

Meanwhile, wrap the heads of chicory in the ham slices and lay them in the sauce. Cover the casserole and simmer gently for about 40 minutes, or until the chicory is tender through to the middle.

Carefully transfer the ham-wrapped chicory to a warmed serving dish. Boil the sauce for 2 minutes then pour it over the vegetables and serve.

Beetroot and Orange Salad

I use honey all the time in salad dressings instead of sugar – it adds a pleasing flavour as well as the sweetness needed to complement the other ingredients. You can make this yogurt dressing for lots of other salads – coleslaw, cucumber salad, Waldorf salad and green salad, for example. Serves 4

Metric		Imperial
6	small beetroot, cooked	6
2	oranges	2
1	small onion	1
	Yogurt dressing	
4 tablespoons	natural yogurt	4 tablespoons
1 tablespoon	clear honey	1 tablespoon
1	clove garlic, crushed	1
	salt and freshly ground black pepper	
	a little grated nutmeg	

Cut the beetroot in half. Grate the rind from one of the oranges and mix it with the beetroot. Cut all the peel and pith from the oranges and slice the fruit. Remove any pips and pith as you do so. Combine the orange slices with the beetroot and transfer to a shallow serving dish or plate. Thinly slice the onion and separate it into rings. Sprinkle these over the salad.

Place all the ingredients for the dressing in a bowl and stir well until thoroughly blended. Pour over the salad and serve.

Sesame Bean Sprout Salad

Roasted sesame seeds and honey are used to flavour the creamy dressing poured over the crunchy vegetables in this delicious salad.

Serves 4

Metric		Imperial
225 g	bean sprouts	8 oz
100 g	young carrots	4 oz
3	stalks celery	3
1	bunch of spring onions	1
	Honey and sesame dressing	
3 tablespoons	sesame seeds	3 tablespoons
2 tablespoons	clear honey	2 tablespoons
1 tablespoon	lemon juice	1 tablespoon
2 teaspoons	mild prepared mustard	2 teaspoons
	salt and freshly ground black pepper	
4 tablespoons	soured cream	4 tablespoons

Rinse and dry the bean sprouts, then place in a large bowl. Cut the carrots and celery into fine julienne strips. Trim the spring onions and cut them into strips. Add the carrots, celery and spring onions to the bean sprouts and toss together well.

In a dry, heavy-based frying pan or small saucepan, roast the sesame seeds over a low heat until they are lightly browned. Remove the pan from the heat and stir in the honey. Stir in the remaining ingredients and pour the dressing over the salad. Toss well and serve.

Brown Rice and Mushroom Salad

Honey and fresh herbs blend to make this simple salad quite delicious; both rice and mushrooms benefit from the well-flavoured dressing and the salad should be left to stand a while for the flavours to mingle. Serves 4

Metric		Imperial
175 g	long-grain brown rice	6 oz
	pared rind of 1 lemon	
	salt and freshly ground black pepper	
225 g	button mushrooms	8 oz
1	bunch of spring onions	1
50 g	flaked almonds	2 oz
	Honey-herb dressing	
2 tablespoons	chopped parsley	2 tablespoons
1 tablespoon	chopped fresh tarragon	1 tablespoon
	few sprigs of thyme	
1 tablespoon	chopped fresh marjoram	1 tablespoon
2 tablespoons	lemon juice	2 tablespoons
3 tablespoons	clear honey	3 tablespoons
4 tablespoons	mayonnaise	4 tablespoons
4 tablespoons	olive or salad oil	4 tablespoons

Cook the rice with the lemon rind in plenty of boiling salted water for about 40–45 minutes, or until the grains are tender but not sticky. Drain and remove the lemon rind.

While the rice is cooking, finely slice the mushrooms and trim and chop the spring onions. Toast the flaked almonds and mix them with the mushrooms and spring onions.

To make the dressing, mix the herbs together. You can substitute dried tarragon and marjoram if you do not have the fresh herbs, but use half the quantities given. Stir the lemon juice and honey into the mayonnaise, then gradually whisk in the oil. Stir in the herbs and season to taste.

As soon as the rice is cooked and drained, turn it into a bowl. Add the mushroom mixture and pour over the dressing. Toss well and set aside, covered, to cool. While the rice is hot it will absorb more flavour from the dressing.

Make sure the salad is well tossed before serving then arrange it on a bed of lettuce or shredded Chinese cabbage, if you like.

Puddings and Desserts

Here the use of honey needs no explanation and the recipes combine traditional favourites, healthy ideas for simple puddings and bright ideas to add to the always welcome new desserts. Lovely hot puds for winter days and light airy creams, mousses and frozen treats, all these are included.

In addition to the recipes given here, honey is the perfect sweetener for soufflé omelettes, pancakes and waffles. For ultra-quick success you can prepare an impressive honey sauce to pour over ice cream simply by adding a little rum, Cointreau or brandy to some clear honey. In fact honey can be used to sweeten and flavour most of your favourite desserts – pies, crumbles, flans and even milk puddings.

There must be a honey dessert suitable for every occasion – whether you are looking for a wholesome pudding to follow Sunday lunch or a delicate treat to bring your dinner party to a glorious finale.

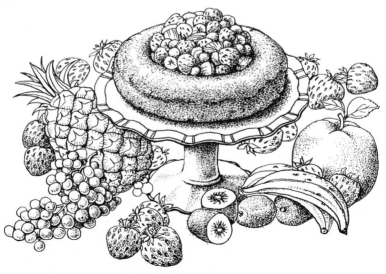

Apple and Blackberry Parcels

(Illustrated on page 103)
Serve these tangy fruit dumplings freshly cooked, with a custard
sauce or cream. Serves 4

Metric		Imperial
350 g	plain flour	12 oz
	pinch of salt	
175 g	margarine	6 oz
	cold water to mix	
	milk and caster sugar to glaze	
	Filling	
4	large cooking apples	4
225 g	blackberries	8 oz
2 tablespoons	set honey	2 tablespoons
2 tablespoons	soft brown sugar	2 tablespoons

Sift the flour into a bowl with the salt. Add the margarine, cut into pieces, and rub it in until the mixture resembles fine breadcrumbs. Add just enough cold water to bind the ingredients together, then form the mixture into a ball. Divide the pastry into four equal portions.

Peel and core the cooking apples. Roll out the pastry into four circles each large enough to enclose an apple. Place one apple on each circle of pastry. Mix the blackberries with the honey and sugar, then spoon them into the middle of the apples. Dampen the edges of the pastry and fold it up around the fruit. Trim off any excess pastry and use it to decorate the dumplings. Seal the edges and place the dumplings sealed side down on a greased baking tray.

Brush lightly with milk and sprinkle a little sugar over. Make a small hole in the top of each dumpling and add any pastry decorations made from the trimmings. Bake in a moderately hot oven (200 C, 400 F, gas 6) for 30 minutes.

Flapjack Fruit Pudding

This pudding is an excellent standby for times when you find that the cupboard is relatively bare, or when you simply don't have time to make the pastry for a fruit pie. You can use any of those fruits which you would use in a pie – apples, rhubarb, raspberries, plums, gooseberries, pears or apricots – but remember to adjust the amount of honey you pour over the fruit according to its sweetness. For example, rhubarb or gooseberries would require more honey than pears or plums. Serves 4

Metric		Imperial
450 g	fresh fruit	1 lb
4–6 tablespoons	clear honey	4–6 tablespoons
100 g	butter or margarine	4 oz
100 g	rolled oats	4 oz
	grated rind of 1 orange	

Prepare the fruit according to its type and place it in an ovenproof dish. Trickle 2–4 tablespoons of the honey over and set the dish aside while you make the topping.

Melt the remaining honey (2 tablespoons) with the butter or margarine. Add the oats and orange rind and mix thoroughly. Spread this oat mixture over the fruit and bake in a moderate oven (180 C, 350 F, gas 4) for 45–60 minutes. Serve hot or warm with custard or cream.

Honeyed Apple Charlotte

This pudding is so economical to prepare and it is really delicious to eat – even better for the additional flavour which the honey gives the apples. Serves 6

Metric		Imperial
about 15	medium slices bread	about 15
100 g	butter	4 oz
1 kg	cooking apples	2 lb
100 g	clear honey	4 oz

Cut the crusts off the bread. You can dry them out and make into breadcrumbs, if you like. Butter the bread slices, then use most of them to neatly line a straight-sided ovenproof dish, buttered side out; one measuring about 20-cm/8-in. in diameter should do – it doesn't matter if the sides of the dish slope, so long as they do not curve then the dish is suitable.

Peel, core and slice the apples. Layer them in the dish, pressing them down well. Trickle the honey over the apples, allowing time for it to run down between the slices. Arrange the remaining buttered bread on top, buttered side up, to cover the apples completely, then bake in a moderate oven (180 C, 350 F, gas 4) for about 1 hour 20 minutes, or until the outside is golden brown.

Turn the charlotte out on to a serving dish and serve immediately with custard sauce or cream. Ice cream also tastes very good with cooked apple dishes!

Fruit Sponge Pudding

Here is a variation on that old favourite, Eve's pudding. The combination of honey and banana with the apples, and chopped hazelnuts on top, gives this idea a new lease of life. Serves 4

Metric		Imperial
450 g	cooking apples	1 lb
1	large banana	1
4 tablespoons	clear honey	4 tablespoons
	grated rind of 1 orange	
	Topping	
50 g	butter or margarine	2 oz
50 g	caster sugar	2 oz
1	egg	1
75 g	self-raising flour	3 oz
	juice of 1 orange	
50 g	hazelnuts, chopped	2 oz
1 tablespoon	clear honey	1 tablespoon

Peel, core and thinly slice the apples, slice the banana and mix both in an ovenproof dish. Pour over the honey and sprinkle with the orange rind.

Cream the butter with the sugar until pale and light. Beat in the egg and fold in the flour with the orange juice. Spread this mixture over the fruit and bake in a moderate oven (180 C, 350 F, gas 4) for 40–45 minutes.

Lightly toast the hazelnuts and warm the honey. Mix together and spread lightly over the cooked pudding. Serve immediately.

Fritters with Honey Rum Sauce

Serve these freshly made fritters with clotted cream as a very special dessert treat. Serves 4

Metric		Imperial
450 g	cooking apples	1 lb
4	large bananas	4
	juice of ½ lemon	
	Honey rum sauce	
4 tablespoons	clear honey	4 tablespoons
2 tablespoons	white rum	2 tablespoons
	grated rind and juice of 1 orange	
150 ml	water	¼ pint
	Batter	
100 g	plain flour	4 oz
2	eggs, separated	2
150 ml	water	¼ pint
	oil for deep frying	

Peel, core and slice the apples into rings. Cut the bananas in half lengthways. Sprinkle the lemon juice over the fruit.

To make the sauce, mix all the ingredients in a small saucepan and heat slowly to boiling point. Leave the pan over very low heat while you prepare the fritters.

First make the batter: sift the flour into a bowl and make a well in the centre. Place the egg yolks and water in the well and gradually beat in the flour to make a smooth batter. Whisk the egg whites until they stand in stiff peaks, then fold them carefully into the batter.

Heat the oil for deep frying to 180 C/350 F. Dip the pieces of fruit in the batter, making sure that they are well coated, then drop them into the hot oil. Cook, turning once, until crisp and golden, then drain on absorbent kitchen paper. Arrange the fritters on a heated serving dish and pour over the hot sauce. Serve immediately.

Apricot Beignets

These choux pastry fritters have to be eaten freshly made. You can prepare the flour paste in advance ready to beat in the eggs and fruit at the last minute. Serve with whipped cream. Serves 4

Metric		Imperial
150 ml	water	$\frac{1}{4}$ pint
65 g	butter	$2\frac{1}{2}$ oz
75 g	plain flour	3 oz
2	eggs, lightly beaten	2
1	425-g/15-oz can apricot halves, drained	1
	oil for deep frying	
2–3	tablespoons clear honey	2–3 tablespoons

Pour the water into a saucepan and add the butter. Heat gently until the butter melts, then bring quickly to the boil. Meanwhile sift the flour into a bowl. Immediately the water and butter mixture boils, remove the pan from the heat and add the flour all at once. Stir it in until the mixture forms a ball of paste. Set aside to cool slightly. When the paste is just warm, beat in the eggs, a little at a time, until the mixture is smooth and very glossy.

Roughly chop the apricots and add them to the paste. Heat the oil for deep frying to 180 C/350 F. Drop spoonfuls of the paste into the hot oil and cook until well puffed and golden brown. Drain on absorbent kitchen paper and keep hot while you fry the remaining mixture.

Heat the honey in a small saucepan over low heat, then pour it over the beignets to sweeten and glaze them just before they are served.

Apple Pancakes

(Illustrated on page 52)
Be prepared to serve second helpings of these pancakes – sweetened
with honey and filled with apples they are bound to be a family
favourite. Serves 4

Metric		Imperial
double quantity	pancake batter (page 20)	double quantity
	butter or oil for cooking	
	Filling	
450 g	cooking apples	1 lb
1 tablespoon	lemon juice	1 tablespoon
50 g	butter	2 oz
4 tablespoons	clear honey	4 tablespoons

Make the pancake batter. While it is standing, peel, core and quarter the apples. Cut the quarters into slices and place them in a bowl. Sprinkle the lemon juice over.

Make the pancakes according to the instructions on page 20. Stack them layered with absorbent kitchen paper and keep hot until the filling is ready.

Melt the butter in a frying pan, add the apple slices and cook, turning once, until browned on both sides. Pour in the honey and heat through for a minute.

To serve, either layer the pancakes with the apples on a serving platter, or top each pancake with a little of the apple and honey mixture, fold over and arrange on a warmed serving plate. Serve immediately.

Almond Honey Puff

Honey is used in quantity in many Greek cakes and desserts. It is often combined with nuts and fine filo pastry to make rich desserts. Here is a recipe which layers puff pastry with almonds and honey for an equally luxurious result. Serves 6

Metric		Imperial
175 g	ground almonds	6 oz
175 g	clear honey	6 oz
1	370-g/13-oz packet frozen puff pastry, thawed	1
	a few drops rose water	
25 g	flaked almonds	1 oz
Rum syrup		
3 tablespoons	clear honey	3 tablespoons
2 tablespoons	white rum	2 tablespoons
2 tablespoons	boiling water	2 tablespoons

Mix the ground almonds with all but 2 teaspoons of the honey. Cut the pastry into four equal portions, then roll out each into a very thin oblong measuring just slightly more than 20 × 30 cm/8 × 12 in. On a greased baking tray, sandwich the sheets of pastry together with the almond and honey paste, spreading it very carefully over the pastry so as not to make any holes. End with a layer of pastry on top and trim the edges with a sharp knife.

Mix the reserved honey with the rosewater and brush this over the pastry. Sprinkle the flaked almonds over and bake in a hot oven (220 C, 425 F, gas 7) for 15–20 minutes, or until the pastry is puffed and browned.

While the puff is cooking, mix the honey, rum and boiling water together. Remove the almond puff from the oven and cut it into six pieces – a sharp serrated bread knife is best for this. Transfer the almond puff to a serving plate and trickle the syrup over. Serve immediately. Alternatively cool the whole almond honey puff on a wire rack, then cut it up and trickle the syrup over to serve.

Honey-fried Bananas

Serves 4

Metric		Imperial
4	bananas	4
	juice of ½ lemon	
50 g	butter	2 oz
25 g	flaked almonds	1 oz
2 tablespoons	clear honey	2 tablespoons

Cut the bananas in half lengthwise and sprinkle the lemon juice over them.
   Melt the butter in a frying pan, add the bananas and cook, turning once, until browned on both sides. Transfer to a warmed serving plate. Add the almonds to the butter remaining in the pan and cook until lightly browned. Stir in the honey and heat through. Pour over the bananas and serve immediately.

Honey-baked Pears

Serve this refreshing dessert with cream or ice cream. Alternatively, you can substitute dry cider for the wine. Serves 4

Metric		Imperial
4	large firm pears	4
	juice of 1 lemon	
4 tablespoons	clear honey	4 tablespoons
150 ml	dry white wine	¼ pint

Peel the pears, leaving their stalks in place. If you like, turn them upside-down and cut out the core. Sprinkle with the lemon juice and arrange them in a small ovenproof dish. Mix the honey with the wine and pour over the pears.
   Bake in a moderate oven (180 C, 350 F, gas 4) for 1 hour, or until the pears are tender. Baste frequently during cooking, then serve the pears hot or lightly chilled.

Honey-mulled Fruits

This fruit salad also makes a pleasant and healthy breakfast dish when served with a little natural yogurt. For dessert, you can present it either hot or cold with cream or yogurt. Serves 4

Metric		Imperial
350 g	dried fruits, for example apricots, prunes, apples, pears, peaches and raisins	12 oz
600 ml	water	1 pint
	pared rind of 1 lemon	
2	cloves	2
1	cinnamon stick	1
4–5 tablespoons	clear honey	4–5 tablespoons

Place the fruits in a bowl and pour over the water. Leave to stand, covered, overnight.

Pour the soaked fruit and the liquid into a saucepan and add the lemon rind, cloves, cinnamon and honey. Add a little extra water if the fruit is not covered with liquid. Heat slowly to boiling point, then reduce the heat and cover the pan. Simmer the fruit for 15–20 minutes.

Taste to make sure that the syrup is sweet enough for your liking, then serve the mulled fruits hot, or cool and chill them before serving.

Baked Cheesecake

Here is a recipe for a traditional, rich cheesecake. Honey lends itself perfectly to flavouring and sweetening such desserts. You can add 50 g/2 oz sultanas to the filling, if you like. Serves 6–8

Metric		Imperial
225 g	plain flour	8 oz
175 g	butter or margarine	6 oz
2 tablespoons	clear honey	2 tablespoons
	Filling	
225 g	cream cheese	8 oz
2	eggs, separated	2
5 tablespoons	clear honey	5 tablespoons
	grated rind and juice of 1 lemon	
2 tablespoons	self-raising flour	2 tablespoons
	generous pinch of ground cinnamon	

Sift the flour into a bowl. Add the butter or margarine, cut into pieces, and rub it in until the mixture resembles breadcrumbs. Stir in the honey and lightly knead the mixture into a pastry dough. Roll out and use to line a 23-cm/9-in flan dish. Bake blind in a moderate oven (180 C, 350 F, gas 4) for 30 minutes. Allow to cool while you prepare the filling.

Beat the cream cheese and egg yolks together. Stir in the honey, lemon rind and juice, then sift the flour and cinnamon over and stir in. Whisk the egg whites until stiff and fold into the cheese mixture to make a frothy batter. Pour this into the flan case and bake for about a further 45 minutes. When the filling is well browned and set, leave the cheesecake to cool completely, then chill it lightly before serving with whipped cream.

Yogurt Cheesecake

Yogurt cheese is available from some health food shops and it is also very easy to make. Once you start making your own yogurt cheese to give the thick, creamy product used in this recipe, you will find many other uses for it and may well start to make it on a regular basis. Curd cheese can also be used in this recipe. Serves 6

Metric		Imperial
225 g	chocolate digestive biscuits	8 oz
75 g	butter or margarine	3 oz
Topping		
	grated rind and juice of 1 large orange	
175 g	yogurt cheese (page 22)	6 oz
2 teaspoons	powdered gelatine	2 teaspoons
3 tablespoons	hot water	3 tablespoons
100 g	clear honey	4 oz
150 ml	double cream	$\frac{1}{4}$ pint
Decoration		
225 g	strawberries, hulled	8 oz

Crush the biscuits finely and evenly. Melt the butter or margarine and stir in the biscuits. Press this mixture into the base of a loose-bottomed 20-cm/8-in flan tin. Place in the refrigerator to chill while you make the topping.

Beat the rind and juice of the orange into the yogurt cheese. Dissolve the gelatine in the hot water, in a basin over a saucepan of simmering water. Meanwhile, stir the honey into the cheese mixture and lightly whip the cream. Stir the dissolved gelatine into the cheesecake mixture and finally fold in the whipped cream. Pour this over the biscuit base and chill until set.

Remove the sides of the tin and place the cheesecake on a serving plate. Arrange the strawberries on top and serve.

Savarin

A traditional savarin, filled with a glorious fresh fruit salad, always makes a breathtaking dessert display. Serve it on a high cake stand and offer with it a bowl of clotted or whipped cream. Serves 6–8

Metric		Imperial
225 g	strong plain flour	8 oz
½ teaspoon	salt	½ teaspoon
250 ml	milk	8 fl oz
2 tablespoons	clear honey	2 tablespoons
15 g	dried yeast	½ oz
4	eggs	4
100 g	butter, melted	4 oz
	Rum syrup	
4 tablespoons	clear honey	4 tablespoons
4 tablespoons	white rum	4 tablespoons
2 tablespoons	boiling water	2 tablespoons
	Fruit salad	
225 g	strawberries, hulled	8 oz
1	dessert apple, cored	1
1	banana	1
2	kiwi fruits, peeled	2
50 g	seedless grapes	2 oz
1	small fresh pineapple	1

Sift the flour into a bowl with the salt. Heat the milk and honey together until just lukewarm. Sprinkle the yeast over the liquid and leave in a warm place until the yeast has dissolved and it has become frothy.

Make a well in the flour and pour in the yeast liquid. Lightly beat the eggs and add them to the liquid with the melted butter. Gradually beat in the flour to make a smooth batter, then continue to beat it for 5 minutes. Cover the bowl and leave the batter in a warm place until it has doubled in volume. Meanwhile, grease a 20-cm/8-in ring tin. Lightly beat the batter and pour it into the tin. Leave in a warm place, covered, until the mixture has risen almost to the top of the tin.

Bake the savarin in a moderately hot oven (200 C, 400 F, gas 6) for 35–40 minutes, then turn out and cool on a wire rack.

Before the savarin cools, mix the ingredients for the rum syrup and spoon about half the syrup over the savarin. Work slowly so that the liquid has time to soak into the cake, and place a plate under the rack to catch any syrup that may drip down.

Now prepare the fruit salad. Halve any large strawberries and place them in a bowl. Slice the apple, banana and kiwi fruits and add to the strawberries with the grapes. Trim and peel the pineapple, cutting away the hard core. Cut the flesh into pieces and add to the fruit salad with any juice. Pour the remaining rum syrup into the fruit and mix well.

Place the savarin on a cake stand or plate and arrange the fruit in the middle. Pour the syrup from the fruit and any collected on the plate over the savarin.

Hazelnut Meringue Cake

This is, in fact, very quick and easy to prepare if you have an electric whisk or food mixer. Serve the cake on the same day as you make it and don't worry about having any left over – it's quite mouth watering and is bound to be eaten up in one go! Serves 4–6

Metric		Imperial
4	egg whites	4
8 tablespoons	clear honey	8 tablespoons
225 g	hazelnuts, ground	8 oz
	Filling	
150 ml	double cream	$\frac{1}{4}$ pint
	icing sugar to dust	

Whisk the egg whites until they stand in stiff peaks. Whisking continuously, gradually trickle in the honey and continue whisking vigorously until the mixture is very stiff and glossy. Fold in the ground hazelnuts.

Line two 20-cm/8-in sandwich tins with non-stick baking parchment. Divide the mixture between the tins and bake in a moderate oven (180 C, 350 F, gas 4) for 40 minutes. Turn one of the meringue layers out on to a serving plate, remove the lining paper and allow to cool.

Whip the cream until stiff, then spread it over the cake. Turn out the second meringue layer, remove the paper and carefully place it on top of the cream. Sprinkle a little icing sugar over and serve.

Strawberry Honey Cups

Fresh summer strawberries are best served as simply as possible. But don't you sometimes feel that it's a bit of a cheat when you present a plain bowl of strawberries to your guests? Well, here's the answer – make some crunchy biscuits cups, fill them with strawberries and glaze them with honey. A small dish of clotted cream will complete this impressive dessert. Serves 4

Metric		Imperial
25 g	butter	1 oz
25 g	sugar	1 oz
1 tablespoon	clear honey	1 tablespoon
25 g	plain flour	1 oz
Filling		
675 g	strawberries, hulled	1½ lb
2 tablespoons	clear honey	2 tablespoons
1 tablespoon	orange liqueur	1 tablespoon

Melt the butter with the sugar and honey in a small saucepan. Grease two or three baking trays. Stir the flour into the melted ingredients. Place small spoonfuls of this mixture well apart on the baking trays – it should make eight. Bake in a moderate oven (180 C, 350 F, gas 4) for 8–10 minutes, or until the biscuits are spread out and golden brown.

While the biscuits are cooking, grease eight patty tins. Remove the baking trays from the oven and leave the biscuits on them for a short while. Test the edge of the biscuits with a knife; if they are set just enough to lift, use a wide palette knife to scoop each off in one go and carefully mould each one into the patty tins. Leave the biscuit cups to cool completely in the patty tins. If you find that some of the biscuits have hardened on the baking trays before you have a chance to remove them, replace the trays in the oven for just 30 seconds to warm the mixture and then try again.

Fill the biscuit cups with the strawberries, cutting any large ones in half. Mix the honey with the orange liqueur and glaze the strawberries with this mixture just before serving them.

From the top: **Quick Raspberry Ripple and Honey and Ginger Ice Cream (both on page 88), Pork Meatloaf (page 36) and Bacon and Mushroom Ramekins (page 21)**

Fresh Fruit and Nut Salad

(Illustrated on page 33)
Brazils, pecan nuts and honey turn a simple fruit salad into
something special. Serve with natural yogurt or cream. Serves 4

Metric		Imperial
50 g	each black and green grapes	2 oz
2	oranges	2
2	dessert apples	2
2	bananas	2
1 tablespoon	lemon juice	1 tablespoon
50 g	brazil nuts	2 oz
50 g	pecan nuts	2 oz
	Honey syrup	
4 tablespoons	clear honey	4 tablespoons
1 tablespoon	brandy	1 tablespoon
150 ml	boiling water	$\frac{1}{4}$ pint

Halve the grapes and remove and discard their pips. Place in a bowl. Grate
and reserve the rind from one of the oranges. Cut all the peel and pith from
the oranges, then, working over a plate, cut between the segments and
remove the orange flesh. Reserve all the juice caught on the plate for the
syrup. Quarter, core and slice the apples. Mix into the grapes with the
orange flesh. Slice the bananas and add to the fruit salad, then sprinkle the
lemon juice over. Chop the brazil nuts and stir them into the salad with the
pecans.

To make the honey syrup, mix the honey with the brandy and boiling
water. Stir in the reserved orange rind and juice, then pour the hot syrup
over the fruit and toss well. Chill for about an hour before serving.

From the top: **Blackcurrant Ice Cream, Honey Ice Cream
with raspberries and Brown Bread Ice Cream (all overleaf)**

Honey Ice Cream

(Illustrated on page 86)
Honey sweetens and flavours vanilla ice cream to give a luscious result. Serve this ice cream in the biscuit cups on page 84, if you like, or just scoop it into glass dishes. Serves 6

Metric		Imperial
1	vanilla pod	1
600 ml	milk	1 pint
2	eggs	2
2	egg yolks	2
175 g	clear honey	6 oz
150 ml	double cream	$\frac{1}{4}$ pint

Split the vanilla pod and place it in a saucepan. Pour in the milk and heat slowly to boiling point. Set aside and leave until the milk is just warm. Strain through a sieve, discard the vanilla pod and return the milk to the saucepan. Heat through until the milk is very warm. Remove from the heat.

Whisk the eggs and egg yolks together in a basin. Gradually pour in the milk and stand the basin over a saucepan of hot water. Stir the custard continuously until it has thickened enough to coat the back of a wooden spoon. Do not allow the water to boil, or overcook the custard, as the eggs will curdle. Set aside to cool, stirring occasionally to prevent a skin forming on the surface.

Warm the honey very slightly, then stir it into the custard. Lightly whip the cream and fold it into the mixture. Pour into a freezer container and place in the freezer or freezing compartment of the refrigerator until half frozen. Thoroughly whisk the slushy ice cream, then return it to the freezer and repeat once more. Finally, leave until firm and then serve.

Variations

Honey and Ginger Ice Cream *(Illustrated on page 85)* Add 100 g/4 oz chopped crystallised ginger to the custard with the honey. Continue as above.

Brown Bread Ice Cream *(Illustrated on page 86)* Add 100 g/4 oz fresh brown breadcrumbs to the custard with the honey. Stir in 4 tablespoons medium or sweet sherry before you fold in the cream.

Quick Raspberry Ripple *(Illustrated on page 85)* Make the ice cream as above. When you are whisking it for the second time, lightly stir through 225 g/8 oz good quality raspberry jam or conserve. Freeze as above.

Blackcurrant Ice Cream *(Illustrated on page 86)* Before you make the ice cream, cook 450 g/1 lb blackcurrants in 4–6 tablespoons water until they are tender and most of the excess liquid has evaporated. Blend in a liquidiser, then press the fruit purée through a sieve.

Make the ice cream as above, stirring the fruit purée in with the honey. Continue as above.

Apricot Mousse

This mousse is very delicately flavoured and light in texture. When fresh apricots are in season, substitute them for the canned ones. Use 450 g/1 lb to mix into the mousse, reserving a few for decoration; first halve, stone and lightly cook them in very little water and honey to taste.
Serves 4–6

Metric		Imperial
2	425-g/15-oz cans apricot halves, drained	2
2	eggs, separated	2
1 tablespoon	caster sugar	1 tablespoon
4 tablespoons	clear honey	4 tablespoons
2 teaspoons	powdered gelatine	2 teaspoons
3 tablespoons	hot water	3 tablespoons
150 ml	double cream	$\frac{1}{4}$ pint

Purée one can of apricots either in a liquidiser or by pressing the fruit through a sieve. Whisk the egg yolks with the caster sugar until pale and creamy. Stir in the apricot purée and honey.

Dissolve the gelatine in the hot water, in a basin over a saucepan of simmering water. Stir the dissolved gelatine into the apricot mixture then put aside until it is just beginning to set. Whip the cream until thick and fold into the mousse. Whisk the egg whites until they stand in stiff peaks, then fold in.

Pour the mousse into a 1.15-litre/2-pint mould and chill until set. Turn out and serve decorated with the remaining apricots.

Honey Syllabub

This is one of the simplest desserts to prepare and it is very rich – so serve it after a light main course. Offer a plate of unfilled Honey Snaps (page 105) with the syllabub. Serves 4

Metric		Imperial
4 tablespoons	clear honey	4 tablespoons
2 tablespoons	dry sherry	2 tablespoons
2 tablespoons	brandy	2 tablespoons
1 tablespoon	fresh orange or lemon juice	1 tablespoon
	grated rind of 1 orange or lemon	
300 ml	double cream	½ pint

Mix the honey with the sherry, brandy and orange or lemon juice in a bowl. Stir in the orange or lemon rind and the cream. Whisk until the mixture becomes thick and light, then spoon it into tall glasses and chill the syllabub thoroughly before serving.

Rhubarb Sorbet

Sorbets are deliciously refreshing on hot summer days or to follow a rich meal. This simple sorbet can be served in the small biscuit cups on page 84. Serves 4–6

Metric		Imperial
450 g	trimmed rhubarb	1 lb
225 g	clear honey	8 oz
2	egg whites	2

Cut the rhubarb into slices and place in a saucepan. Add 2 tablespoons of the honey and heat gently until the juice runs from the fruit. Bring to the boil, then reduce the heat and simmer gently, covered, for about 20 minutes, or until the fruit is very soft and pulpy. Cool slightly.

Purée the fruit in a liquidiser until quite smooth, then transfer it to a freezer container. Whisk in the honey and place in the freezer until half frozen. When the sorbet is slushy, remove it from the freezer and whisk it thoroughly. Whisk the egg whites until they stand in stiff peaks, then fold them into the rhubarb mixture. Freeze until firm.

Serve scoops of the sorbet in glass dishes.

Quick Yogurt and Honey Desserts

A small glass of chilled yogurt, sweetened to taste with clear honey and sprinkled with chopped nuts makes a quick, healthy and most refreshing dessert. However, if you would like to make your hurried dessert surprises a little more imaginative, try some of the following ideas. Each one serves four.

Banana Whizz
Place 2 large, sliced bananas, 300 ml/½ pint chilled natural yogurt and 4 tablespoons set honey in a liquidiser and blend until smooth. Pour into four individual glasses and swirl 1 tablespoon double cream in each. Top with toasted chopped hazelnuts and serve with small biscuits, if you like.

Fruit and Nut Yogurt
Mix 50 g/2 oz raisins with 50 g/2 oz toasted flaked almonds, 2 cored and chopped dessert apples and the grated rind of 1 orange. Divide this mixture between four individual glass dishes and top each with 150 ml/¼ pint natural yogurt. Trickle 1 tablespoon clear honey over each and serve.

Quick Melon Cooler
Halve 1 ripe honeydew melon and scoop out the seeds. Scoop out all the flesh, preferably with a melon baller, then return it to the shell, dividing it equally between the two halves. Mix 2 tablespoons chopped preserved ginger and 3 tablespoons clear honey into 300 ml/½ pint well-chilled natural yogurt. Pour this over the melon halves, toss lightly and serve.

Tropical Delight
Mix 1 (439-g/15½-oz) can pineapple bits with 2 peeled and chopped kiwi fruits, 1 (312-g/11-oz) can lychees (drained) and 4 tablespoons clear honey. Layer this fruit mixture in a bowl with 600 ml/1 pint chilled natural yogurt. Top with a little toasted desiccated coconut and serve.

Yogurt Brûlée
Whip 300 ml/½ pint chilled natural yogurt with 300 ml/½ pint double cream. Pour into an ovenproof dish and swirl 4 tablespoons clear honey over the top. Sprinkle 25 g/1 oz flaked almonds over and place under a hot grill until caramelised and bubbling. Serve immediately.

Baking

Honey contributes a warming flavour to home-baked cakes and biscuits, and its water-attracting properties mean that it gives moist results – cakes and breads keep better when made with honey.

Included in this chapter is a selection of baking recipes – from moist light cakes and delicate biscuits to wholesome teabread and delicious home-baked bread. You can include a little honey in many of your favourite cake and bread recipes: add small quantities for a moist result and use slightly less sugar to compensate. Use it also in sweet pastry recipes instead of water.

When you bake with honey you will surely be pleased with the well-flavoured results, as too will your family – you may even find that you end up making more cakes than ever before!

Raisin Teabread

Here is a recipe for a simple teabread – it can be varied by adding nuts, other dried fruits and your favourite spices. Makes one 1-kg/2-lb loaf

Metric		Imperial
225 g	raisins	8 oz
75 g	set honey	3 oz
300 ml	freshly made strong tea	$\frac{1}{2}$ pint
2	eggs, lightly beaten	2
275 g	wholewheat flour	10 oz
$\frac{1}{2}$ teaspoon	ground mixed spice	$\frac{1}{2}$ teaspoon
3 teaspoons	baking powder	3 teaspoons

Place the raisins in a bowl. Stir the honey into the tea and pour this over the raisins. Leave to soak for 2 hours. Stir the eggs into the raisin mixture.

Mix the flour with the spice and baking powder, then mix these dry ingredients into the raisin mixture. Transfer to a greased 1-kg/2-lb loaf tin and bake in a moderate oven (180 C, 350 F, gas 4) for about 1 hour 10 minutes. When cooked, a metal skewer inserted into the teabread will come out clean of mixture.

Cool on a wire rack and serve sliced and buttered.

Variations

Date and Walnut Teabread Substitute 100 g/4 oz chopped cooking dates for the raisins and add 100 g/4 oz chopped walnuts to the mixture with the dry ingredients.

Malted Raisin Teabread Stir 1 tablespoon malt extract into the tea with the honey. Continue as above.

Honey Wholewheat Loaf

*The addition of honey to bread gives a slight sweetness which brings
out the nutty flavour of the wholewheat flour to make a superb loaf.
Makes one 675-g/1½-lb loaf*

Metric		Imperial
3 tablespoons	set honey	3 tablespoons
	lukewarm water	
1½ teaspoons	dried yeast	1½ teaspoons
450 g	wholewheat flour	1 lb
½ teaspoon	salt	½ teaspoon
50 g	butter, melted	2 oz
	Topping	
	beaten egg to brush	
	sesame seeds, poppy seeds or nibbed wheat	

Dissolve the honey in a little warm water in a measuring jug, then make up
to 300 ml/½ pint with more lukewarm water. Sprinkle the yeast over the
surface of the liquid and leave it in a warm place until the yeast has
dissolved and the liquid is frothy.

Mix the flour with the salt in a bowl. Make a well in the centre and pour
in the frothy yeast liquid and melted butter. Mix the liquid into the dry
ingredients to make a firm dough. Knead the dough thoroughly on a lightly
floured surface for about 10 minutes or until it feels smooth and elastic.
Place in a lightly oiled bowl and cover with cling film. Leave in a warm place
until doubled in size – this may take several hours.

Turn out the risen dough on to a floured surface and lightly knead it.
Shape into a simple round loaf and place it on a greased baking tray. Cover
with oiled cling film and leave in a warm place until almost doubled in size.

If you like, you can be a little more adventurous in shaping the bread.
Try making a plait for example – divide the dough into three equal
portions, roll these into long sausage shapes of equal length, then plait
them together. Make sure that the ends are neatly tucked in and place the
loaf on a greased baking tray. Leave to rise as above.

To make a cottage loaf, cut off about one-third of the dough. Shape the
larger portion into a simple round loaf and place it on a greased baking
tray. Shape the smaller portion into a ball, brush the top of the loaf with a
little water and press the ball of dough on to it. Make an indentation
in the middle of the loaf with your thumb, then leave to rise as above.

When the loaf has risen, brush it with a little beaten egg and sprinkle
some sesame seeds, poppy seeds or nibbed wheat over the top. Bake in a
hot oven (220 C, 425 F, gas 7) for 30–40 minutes. When cooked the loaf will
sound hollow if tapped on the bottom. Cool on a wire rack.

Variation

To make bread rolls, shape small portions of the dough into rounds, plaits or tiny cottage loaves (as shown on front cover). Leave to rise, glaze and bake as above for about 15 minutes.

Fruit and Nut Cake

This cake has excellent keeping qualities – that is if you can keep it from the family! To make a very special cake you can always add 50 g/2 oz crystallised pineapple, a few pieces of crystallised ginger and about 50 g/2 oz chopped brazil nuts to the ingredients.
Makes one 23-cm/9in cake

Metric		Imperial
175 g	butter or margarine	6 oz
175 g	clear honey	6 oz
100 g	caster sugar	4 oz
3	eggs, lightly beaten	3
350 g	self-raising flour	12 oz
1 teaspoon	baking powder	1 teaspoon
75 g	raisins	3 oz
75 g	sultanas	3 oz
50 g	cut mixed peel	2 oz
75 g	walnut pieces	3 oz
	grated rind of 1 orange	

Cream the butter or margarine with the honey and sugar until light and soft. Gradually beat in the eggs, adding a little flour to prevent the mixture curdling.

Sift the remaining flour with the baking powder over the mixture and fold in gently. Mix the remaining ingredients together and fold them into the cake. Transfer to a greased and lined 23-cm/9-in cake tin and bake in a moderate oven (160 C, 325 F, gas 3) for about 2–2¼ hours. Cover the cake loosely with a piece of cooking foil if it becomes too dark during cooking. When the cake is cooked, a metal skewer inserted into the middle should come out clean of mixture.

Turn out and cool the cake on a wire rack. Remove the paper when the cake is cold.

Honey Madeira Cake

The honey in this recipe gives a moist, well-flavoured result. Makes
one 1-kg/2-lb cake

Metric		Imperial
175 g	butter	6 oz
100 g	set honey	4 oz
75 g	caster sugar	3 oz
	grated rind of 1 lemon	
3	eggs, lightly beaten	3
250 g	self-raising flour	9 oz
	Glaze (optional)	
1 tablespoon	clear honey	1 tablespoon
2 tablespoons	chopped blanched almonds, toasted	2 tablespoons

Cream the butter with the honey and sugar until soft, pale and light. Mix in
the lemon rind and gradually beat in the eggs, adding a little of the flour as
you do so to prevent the mixture curdling.

Sift the flour over the mixture and fold it in gently. Transfer the cake
mixture to a greased and base-lined 1-kg/2-lb loaf tin. Bake in a moderate
oven (160 C, 325 F, gas 3) for about 1 hour 10 minutes to 1 hour 15 minutes.
When the cake is cooked, a metal skewer inserted into the middle should
come out clean of mixture.

Cool the cake on a wire rack. If you would like to glaze the cake, warm
the clear honey in a small saucepan and brush it over the cooled cake.
Sprinkle with the toasted almonds and leave for 5 minutes before serving.

Honey and Lemon Sponge

For special occasions or for dessert, you can fill this cake with fresh
fruit – strawberries or raspberries, for example – and whipped cream.
Top with more whipped cream and sprinkle some toasted flaked
almonds over. Makes one 20-cm/8-in cake

Metric		Imperial
3	eggs	3
100 g	caster sugar	4 oz
75 g	plain flour	3 oz
3 tablespoons	clear honey	3 tablespoons
	grated rind of 1 lemon	
	Filling	
150 ml	double cream	$\frac{1}{4}$ pint
2 tablespoons	clear honey	2 tablespoons
	Icing	
225 g	icing sugar	8 oz
2–3 tablespoons	lemon juice	2–3 tablespoons
	pared and shredded rind of 1 lemon (optional)	

Whisk the eggs with the sugar until thick and creamy. Sift the flour over and fold it in carefully together with the honey and lemon rind. Trickle the honey over gently so that it is gradually folded into the whisked mixture. Do not stir the mixture or you will knock out all the air.

Pour into two base-lined and greased 20-cm/8-in sandwich tins. Bake in a moderate oven (180 C, 350 F, gas 4) for 25–30 minutes. Turn out and cool on a wire rack.

Whip the cream with the honey until thick. Sift the icing sugar into a bowl, then gradually beat in the lemon juice to make a glacé icing which will pour over the cake.

Sandwich the cooled cakes together with the cream, then pour the icing over the top. If you like, decorate with a little shredded lemon rind, cooked in boiling water until soft, then drained and cooled.

Honey Roll

Here is a variation on a Swiss roll. Honey is particularly useful for flavouring such light sponge cakes and delicate mixtures. Serves 6–8

Metric		Imperial
3	eggs	3
100 g	clear honey	4 oz
100 g	caster sugar	4 oz
100 g	self-raising flour	4 oz
	icing sugar to dust	
	Filling	
150 ml	double cream	$\frac{1}{4}$ pint
1 tablespoon	clear honey	1 tablespoon

Whisk the eggs with the honey and sugar until the mixture is pale, thick and creamy. Sift the flour twice, then fold it very gently into the whisked mixture. Take great care not to stir the mixture or you will knock out all the air which was incorporated during whisking. Use a metal spoon and make a cutting and folding action.

Pour into a lined and greased 23 × 33-cm/9 × 13-in Swiss roll tin. Bake in a hot oven (220 C, 425 F, gas 7) for about 12 minutes, or until the sponge is risen, set and well browned.

Have ready a teatowel with a sheet of greaseproof paper laid on top. Turn the cake out on to the paper and peel off the paper from baking. Trim off the crisp edges of the cake and lay a second sheet of greaseproof on top. Roll up to enclose one sheet of paper in the middle, using the second sheet and the teatowel as a guide. Leave the cake wrapped for half a minute, then remove the teatowel and cool the roll on a wire rack.

Whip the cream with the honey. Unroll the cake and spread the cream filling over the inside. Roll up, sprinkle with a little icing sugar and serve.

Honey and Almond Doughnuts

If you like doughnuts you'll love these! Serve them warm and you will find that you can eat more doughnuts than you had ever imagined possible! For a filling dessert make very small doughnuts from this mixture, fry them and serve with warmed honey poured over and a bowl of whipped cream. Makes 8

Metric		Imperial
225 g	strong plain flour	8 oz
	generous pinch of salt	
150 ml	lukewarm water	$\frac{1}{4}$ pint
1 teaspoon	caster sugar	1 teaspoon
1 teaspoon	dried yeast	1 teaspoon
50 g	butter, melted	2 oz
	oil for deep frying	
	Filling	
50 g	ground almonds	2 oz
25 g	blanched almonds, finely chopped	1 oz
4 tablespoons	set honey	4 tablespoons

Sift the flour into a bowl with the salt. Make a well in the centre and set aside.

Pour the water into a bowl, stir in the sugar and sprinkle the yeast over the top. Leave in a warm place until frothy. Stir the yeast liquid and melted butter into the well in the flour, then mix together to form a dough. Knead thoroughly on a floured surface for about 10 minutes or until the dough feels smooth and elastic. Put into an oiled bowl, cover with cling film and leave in a warm place until doubled in size.

Meanwhile, mix the ingredients for the filling together to make a soft paste. Lightly knead the risen dough and divide it into eight equal portions. Knead and flatten each portion of dough in the palms of your hands. Place some of the filling in the middle and fold the dough up around it, pinching the mixture together to enclose the honey and almonds completely. Place the doughnuts on an oiled baking tray, cover with oiled cling film and leave in a warm place until doubled in size.

Heat the oil for deep frying to 180 c / 350 f. Add the doughnuts and cook, turning occasionally, until they are well browned all over. Drain on absorbent kitchen paper and serve warm or cold.

Apricot Squares

Honey can be used particularly successfully to flavour cakes which are prepared by the melted method as, for example, in this recipe.
Makes 24

Metric		Imperial
175 g	set honey	6 oz
175 g	butter or margarine	6 oz
75 g	caster sugar	3 oz
100 g	dried apricots, chopped	4 oz
2	eggs, lightly beaten	2
225 g	self-raising flour	8 oz
1 teaspoon	baking powder	1 teaspoon
25 g	flaked almonds	1 oz

Melt the honey with the butter or margarine, sugar and apricots in a small saucepan over low heat. Allow to cool slightly before stirring in the eggs. Sift the flour and baking powder together and mix into the melted ingredients.

Pour into a base-lined and greased tin measuring about 19 × 34 cm/7½ × 13½ in. Sprinkle the flaked almonds over the top, then bake in a moderate oven (160 C, 325 F, gas 3) for about 45 minutes or until well risen and browned on top. Cool on a wire rack, then cut into squares to serve.

Fruity Flapjacks

These biscuits are very quick and simple to prepare for a tea-time treat. You can also add grated orange rind and a few chopped nuts (walnuts or hazelnuts) to the mixture if you like. Makes 16

Metric		Imperial
100 g	set honey	4 oz
75 g	butter or margarine	3 oz
50 g	raisins	2 oz
25 g	glacé cherries, chopped	1 oz
25 g	cut mixed peel	1 oz
175 g	rolled oats	6 oz

Melt the honey with the butter or margarine. Stir in the raisins, cherries and peel, then add the oats. Mix thoroughly to combine all the ingredients.

Grease a tin measuring about 19 × 34 cm/7½ × 13½ in and press the mixture into it. Bake in a moderate oven (180 C, 350 F, gas 4) for 30 minutes. Allow the flapjack to stand in the tin until half cooled, then cut it into fingers or squares and remove from the tin. Cool completely on a wire rack.

Honeyed Oatcakes

These semi-sweet biscuits melt in your mouth and they are absolutely delicious with cheese – what better way to round off a meal? Alternatively, serve them with a matured English Cheddar and a glass of refreshingly chilled cider or beer for a wholesome lunchtime snack. Makes about 24

Metric		Imperial
225 g	fine or medium oatmeal	8 oz
50 g	plain flour	2 oz
¼ teaspoon	salt	¼ teaspoon
1 teaspoon	baking powder	1 teaspoon
75 g	butter	3 oz
3 tablespoons	set honey	3 tablespoons

Mix the oatmeal with the flour, salt and baking powder in a bowl. Rub in the butter and mix in the honey to make a biscuit dough.

Take small portions of the mixture – they should be about the size of large walnuts. Roll these first into balls, then flatten them to form neat, thin biscuits. Place the oatcakes on greased baking trays and bake in a moderate oven (180 C, 350 F, gas 4) for 10–12 minutes. Allow to cool slightly on the baking trays, then transfer to wire racks to cool completely. Store in an airtight tin.

Honey Cinnamon Biscuits

Homemade biscuits are so much nicer than most of those you can buy
– so it's well worth the effort of making them. Don't forget that the
cooked, un-iced biscuits will freeze successfully, so if you're in the
mood why not bake a large batch for the freezer? Makes 20

Metric		Imperial
100 g	plain flour	4 oz
75 g	butter	3 oz
$\frac{1}{4}$ teaspoon	ground cinnamon	$\frac{1}{4}$ teaspoon
3 tablespoons	set honey	3 tablespoons
	Icing	
225 g	icing sugar	8 oz
1 tablespoon	clear honey	1 tablespoon
	lemon juice	
	pared rind of 1 lemon (optional)	

Sift the flour into a bowl and rub in the butter. Add the cinnamon and mix in the honey to make a soft biscuit dough. Shape the dough into a roll measuring about 20 cm/8 in. in length and wrap it in cling film. Chill until firm.

Cut the roll of dough into 20 slices and place them slightly apart on greased baking trays. Bake in a moderately hot oven (190 C, 375 F, gas 5) for about 12–15 minutes. Cool slightly on the tray, then transfer the biscuits to a wire rack to cool completely.

To make the icing, sift the icing sugar into a bowl. Gradually beat in the honey and enough lemon juice to make a thick glacé icing. Spread a little over each biscuit and leave to set. Decorate the biscuits with fine strips of boiled lemon rind (see page 97) if you like.

Apple and Blackberry Parcels (page 71)

Honey Snaps

Serve these cream-filled biscuits with coffee or tea, or serve them
unfilled to accompany creamy desserts and ice creams. Makes 6

Metric		Imperial
25 g	butter	1 oz
25 g	sugar	1 oz
2 tablespoons	clear honey	2 tablespoons
2 tablespoons	plain flour	2 tablespoons
	Filling	
75 ml	double cream	3 fl oz
1 tablespoon	clear honey	1 tablespoon

Melt the butter with the sugar and honey. Stir in the flour. Place small spoonfuls of this mixture well apart on greased baking trays. Bake in a moderate oven (180 C, 350 F, gas 4) for 7–9 minutes, or until the biscuits are spread, thin and golden brown.

While the biscuits are cooking, grease the handles of as many wooden spoons as you can find – you will need at least two to roll the biscuits.

Remove the biscuits from the oven and allow them to cool on the trays for a few seconds. Carefully slide a palette knife under them, then wrap the honey snaps around the greased wooden spoon handles. Allow to cool and set before you slide the biscuits off the spoon.

Whip the cream with the honey and pipe it into the biscuits. Serve within an hour of filling.

Note: The quantities given in this recipe are small as it is easier to make these biscuits in small numbers if you are unfamiliar with the technique of baking and rolling them. However, the mixture is very quick to prepare and once the oven is hot you will find that it takes no time at all to make a second or third batch.

From the top: **Chocolate Honey Krispies (page 108),**
Fruit 'n' Nut Clusters (page 110) and Toasted Coconut
Treats (page 111)

Honey Shortbread

These melt-in-the-mouth biscuits are very easy to prepare. You can add almond essence or chopped walnuts to the mixture, as you like.
Makes 24

Metric		Imperial
225 g	butter	8 oz
6 tablespoons	set honey	6 tablespoons
275 g	plain flour	10 oz

Cream the butter with the honey until very soft – the mixture will not become light and fluffy but it must be thoroughly creamed. Sift the flour and stir into the butter mixture.

Press the soft dough into a greased tin measuring about 19 × 34 cm/7½ × 13½ in. Chill thoroughly, then prick the dough all over with a fork, making a neat pattern. Bake in a moderate oven (160 C, 325 F, gas 3) for about 40 minutes, or until the biscuits are pale golden and cooked. Cut into fingers and leave in the tin to cool for a few minutes. When the fingers are firm enough to remove from the tin transfer them to a wire rack to cool.

Wholewheat Hazelnut Biscuits

These biscuits can also be made from walnuts and you may like to add grated orange rind to vary the flavour. Makes about 24.

Metric		Imperial
225 g	butter or margarine	8 oz
5 tablespoons	clear honey	5 tablespoons
250 g	wholewheat flour	9 oz
75 g	hazelnuts, chopped	3 oz

Cream the butter with the honey until the mixture is very soft. The texture will remain buttery; it will become very soft but not light and fluffy. Gradually stir in the flour and nuts to make a soft dough.

Grease an oblong baking tin measuring about 19 × 34 cm/7½ × 13½ in. Press the biscuit mixture into the tin and leave in the refrigerator until it becomes firm. Prick the dough all over with a fork, making a neat pattern, and bake in a moderate oven (160 C, 325 F, gas 3) for 45–50 minutes.

Cut the mixture into fingers while it is in the tin, then carefully transfer the biscuits to a wire rack and allow them to cool completely.

Sweets and Treats

There are times when we all feel the need for a little something – something sweet and indulgent. Perhaps you want to make a small gift for a friend, or a treat to serve with after-dinner coffee? Well, here are a few ideas for simply made sweets, all using honey instead of pounds of sugar.

Treats don't have to be complicated confectionery; try making some cinnamon toast with honey and if you don't already have toast with honey then try that too – such a firm favourite and full of goodness for breakfast or a tea-time snack. One of the nicest indulgences for many people is just a simple spoonful of honey. So next time you want to prepare a surprise for the family, just take out the jar of honey and try a few of these ideas.

Chocolate Honey Krispies

(Illustrated on page 104)
Makes about 64

Metric		Imperial
100 g	set honey	4 oz
100 g	butter	4 oz
¼ teaspoon	almond essence	¼ teaspoon
100 g	Rice Krispies	4 oz
225 g	plain chocolate	8 oz

Melt the honey with the butter and almond essence in a bowl over a saucepan of hot water. Stir in the Rice Krispies and press the mixture into a 20-cm/8-in square tin. Chill until firm.

Melt the chocolate in a basin over a saucepan of hot water. Spread the melted chocolate over the honey mixture and leave until set. Using a hot knife, cut the mixture into small squares and serve on a doily-lined plate.

Honey Popcorn

Popcorn, a great American favourite, makes a delicious, quite nutritious snack. Try tossing a little clear honey into the freshly cooked popcorn – it's scrumptious!

Honey Truffles

Makes 20

Metric		Imperial
100 g	set honey	4 oz
100 g	butter	4 oz
100 g	plain chocolate	4 oz
100 g	blanched almonds	4 oz

Melt the honey, butter and chocolate together in a basin over a saucepan of simmering water. Stir well, then cool and chill until the mixture is firm enough to shape into balls.

Meanwhile, chop the almonds and toast them very lightly and evenly. Using wet hands, shape the chocolate mixture into small balls and roll them in the almonds. Chill until firm and store in the refrigerator.

Honey Hazelnut Cups

These honey chocolates are a little time consuming to prepare, but they really are worth the trouble. Make them for a very special gift or serve them with coffee after dinner. Makes 12

Metric		Imperial
225 g	dark plain chocolate	8 oz
12	hazelnuts	12
about 4 tablespoons	clear honey	about 4 tablespoons

Melt the chocolate in a basin over a saucepan of hot water. Do not allow the water to boil or it may overheat the chocolate.

Have ready 12 double paper sweet cases on a baking tray. Brush the inside of the cases with the melted chocolate, allowing it to cool and set before applying a second and third coat to build up an even case of chocolate inside the cups. Depending on the texture of the chocolate, you may have to brush on several layers. Leave in a cool place to set.

Place a hazelnut in each of the chocolate cups, then pour in about 1 teaspoon of honey. Allow a space between the honey and the rim of the chocolate. Place the cups in the freezer or freezing compartment of the refrigerator for about 10 minutes, or until the chocolate is really firm and the honey quite chilled.

Top the cups with more melted chocolate, making sure that the honey is sealed in. Place in a cool place and leave until completely set. Remove the paper cases and arrange the chocolates in a small gift box, or on a plate.

Honeycomb Brittle

Makes one 20-cm/8-in square slab

Metric		Imperial
225 g	clear honey	8 oz
150 ml	water	$\frac{1}{4}$ pint
	generous pinch of bicarbonate of soda	

Mix the honey and water in a saucepan and heat slowly to boiling point. Boil hard, stirring frequently, until the mixture reaches 138–140 c/280–285 F. Remove the pan from the heat and stir in the bicarbonate of soda. Pour the toffee into a greased 20-cm/8-in square tin and leave until hard. Break into pieces when it is quite cold and store the honeycomb brittle in an airtight tin.

Fruit 'n' Nut Clusters

(Illustrated on page 104)
These little sweets are simple to make, delicious to eat and offer more
in the way of food value than a simple bar of chocolate.
Makes about 24

Metric		Imperial
100 g	plain chocolate	4 oz
100 g	set honey	4 oz
175 g	walnuts	6 oz
100 g	glacé cherries	4 oz
50 g	raisins	2 oz
	grated rind of 1 orange	

Melt the chocolate and honey together in a basin over a saucepan of hot
water. Roughly chop the walnuts and cherries, then mix them with the
raisins and orange rind.

Stir the dried fruit mixture into the melted ingredients, then chill until
the mixture is firm enough to mould into clusters. Place each sweet in a
paper case and chill until firm.

Creamy Fruit and Nut Slice

Serve these sweet cream cheese fingers with coffee instead of a dessert,
or simply make them for a special in-between-meal treat. Makes 18

Metric		Imperial
50 g	glacé cherries	2 oz
100 g	hazelnuts	4 oz
225 g	cream cheese	8 oz
2 teaspoons	cut mixed peel	2 teaspoons
2 tablespoons	set honey	2 tablespoons
	rice paper	

Chop the cherries and nuts. lightly toast the hazelnuts under a hot grill,
taking care not to burn them. Mix the nuts into the cheese with the
cherries, peel and honey.

Line the base of a small oblong tin or 1-kg/2-lb loaf tin with rice paper.
Spread the mixture in the tin and cover with rice paper. Weight down and
chill overnight. Next day, turn out and cut into fingers. Serve chilled.

Toasted Coconut Treats

(Illustrated on page 104)
These are ideal for children to prepare as long as there is an adult
present to supervise the grilling process. Makes about 24

Metric		Imperial
2	egg whites	2
225 g	desiccated coconut	8 oz
4 tablespoons	set honey	4 tablespoons
	pink food colouring (optional)	

Place the egg whites in a bowl and gradually mix in the coconut and honey to make a stiff mixture which can be moulded between the fingers. Shape the mixture into small balls about the size of walnuts. If you wet your hands first you will find that the mixture doesn't stick to your fingers. When you have shaped half the mixture you can add a little pink food colouring to the remainder.

Place the coconut shapes on a greased baking tray or greased foil-lined grill pan and toast under a hot grill until lightly browned. Turn once or twice during cooking to cook all sides. Cool the treats on a wire rack and serve them on a doily-lined plate.

Honey Cinnamon Toast

Here is a special treat for cold winter afternoons. Serves 4

Metric		Imperial
75 g	butter	3 oz
1 tablespoon	set honey	1 tablespoon
½ teaspoon	ground cinnamon	½ teaspoon
4	thick slices bread	4

Cream the butter with the honey and cinnamon. Toast the bread on both sides and spread the honey butter over. Eat at once.

Drinks

Whenever you think of drinks and honey, then mead must surely spring to mind. Probably the oldest alcoholic drink, mead was imbibed by rich and poor alike. It was not just one type of wine – many meads were brewed, each with its own delicate flavour and special characteristics. The drink could be dry or sweet, sparkling or still. We can buy mead at the wine merchants but there is no longer the range of different varieties on offer. If you enjoy making your own wine, then you may like to have a go at mead – homemade mead really can taste excellent.

From alcoholic drinks to medicinal potions: 'honey the healer' comes into its own when you have a sore throat, bad cough or troublesome cold. Honey and lemon must be one of the simplest and best-loved combinations for giving the children. For adults whisky toddies offer enormous comfort when cold symptoms flare. A mixture of honey and cider vinegar can also be taken by the spoonful, or used as the basis for a gargle.

When you're feeling fit and full of fun, try a honey cocktail. There are several drinks in this chapter for parties and gatherings or, if you simply want a cool summer drink, then try making honey lemonade.

Warming and soothing or cooling and refreshing – honey can be used in drinks of all types and for all moods.

Honey Lemonade

This is a wonderfully refreshing drink for hot summer days. Store it in the refrigerator and serve with plenty of ice and a few slices of lemon floating on top. Makes about 1.4 litres/2½ pints

Metric		Imperial
	pared rind and juice of 4 lemons	
1.15 litres	water	2 pints
about 6 tablespoons	clear honey	about 6 tablespoons

Place the lemon rind and juice in a saucepan, add the water and bring slowly to the boil. Remove from the heat and leave until completely cold.

Strain the lemonade and gradually stir in the honey until dissolved. Chill thoroughly before serving.

Spiced Apple Juice

Serve this warming drink as an alternative to alcoholic punches at parties, or have a glass with some hot buttered toast on cold winter afternoons. Serves 6

Metric		Imperial
1	large lemon	1
12	cloves	12
3–4 tablespoons	clear honey	3–4 tablespoons
1	cinnamon stick	1
3	cardamoms	3
1.15 litres	apple juice	2 pints

Wash the lemon and stud it with the cloves. Place the honey in a saucepan and add the cinnamon and cardamoms. Pour in the apple juice, stirring to mix in the honey, and add the lemon. Cover the pan and heat very gently for about an hour. Stir the apple juice occasionally, do not allow it to boil, and cool slightly before serving.

Mead

Mead, a drink that can take on many different characteristics, is one of the oldest of alcoholic beverages. In its different forms it has been, over the centuries, consumed by both peasants and kings alike. For a good mead it is essential that the honey used is of reliable quality. The result can be either sweet or dry depending on the amount of honey used – about 1.5 kg/3 lb for a dry wine and 1.75 kg/4 lb for a sweet wine. As with all other home wine making, it is essential that you sterilise your equipment first – fermentation jars, syphons, filter vessels, all should be thoroughly cleaned with a solution of campden tablets and water. Check that you have prepared all your jars and bottles before starting. Makes 4.5 litres/1 gallon

Metric		Imperial
1.5–1.75 kg	set honey	3–4 lb
600 ml	cold tea	1 pint
	campden tablets	
	boiled water	
1 teaspoon	citric acid	1 teaspoon
	wine yeast compound *or*	
	special mead yeast and yeast nutrient	

Dissolve the honey over low heat, then mix it with the tea and a solution of 1 campden tablet dissolved in 150 ml/¼ pint boiling water. Place in a sterilised 4.5-litre/1-gallon fermentation vessel. Top up to almost three-quarters full with boiled water and shake to mix thoroughly. Add the citric acid and set aside.

Prepare the must – the yeast mixture – according to the instructions given on the packet of yeast or yeast compound. For this mixture you can use either a general wine-making yeast compound which is usually stirred into a small quantity of water and allowed to become frothy before it is added to the fermentation vessel, or you can use a yeast which is particularly suited to making mead. Again this should be dissolved in a small quantity of lukewarm water with about 1 teaspoon yeast nutrient. When the must has been left to ferment for about 3–5 hours it should be added to the fermentation vessel.

Shake the jar well to ensure that all the ingredients are mixed and top up with more cooled, boiled water. Fit a suitable fermentation lock and place the jar in a warm place for the mead to ferment. Keep an eye on your brew to make sure that it is working successfully. If a very heavy sediment builds up quickly, then syphon the mead into a separate vessel, taking just a little of the sediment, and continue the fermentation. When fermentation is complete (about 4-6 weeks), syphon the mead off into a clean, sterilised jar. Do not transfer any of the sediment with the wine.

Again reading the instructions on the packet, dissolve one or two campden tablets in a little hot water and add to the mead. This will ensure that all fermentation ceases and the wine clears. Leave the jar, sealed with an air lock, until the wine has cleared and a sediment has formed. Syphon it off again into another cleaned jar. This process of racking the wine should continue until the mead is clear. If you have a filter kit you can pass the mead through it to give a clear result.

Bottle the mead in sterilised bottles, cork and label them. Store for at least 6 months – the longer homemade wines are stored the better they will taste.

Cool Fruit Cup

If you want to make this drink very impressive, decorate the jug, bowl or glasses with plenty of fruit – slices of kiwi fruit, orange and lemon, and maraschino cherries, for example. Serves 6

Metric		Imperial
4 tablespoons	clear honey	4 tablespoons
	juice of 4 oranges	
2	grapefruit	2
1.15 litres	pineapple juice	2 pints
	ice cubes	
1	lemon	1

Mix the honey with the orange juice in a punch bowl or jug. Grate the rind from the grapefruit, squeeze out their juice and stir both into the honey mixture. Pour in the pineapple juice and add plenty of ice. Slice the lemon, cut the slices in half and stir them into the drink. Allow the fruit cup to stand for 5 minutes before serving.

Honeyed Ginger Beer

Making your own ginger beer is fun and much cheaper than buying lots of fizzy drinks during the summer months.
Makes 4.5 litres / 1 gallon

Metric		Imperial
	To start the brew	
about 8 tablespoons	clear honey	about 8 tablespoons
about 8 tablespoons	ground ginger	about 8 tablespoons
300 ml	lukewarm water	½ pint
25 g	dried yeast	1 oz
	To complete the ginger beer	
350 g	clear honey	12 oz
100 g	sugar	4 oz
	juice of 3 lemons	
about 3.5 litres	water	about 6 pints

To start the ginger beer, ferment the ginger with the yeast and honey in what is known as the 'ginger beer plant'.

Place 2 tablespoons of the honey in a large jar with 2 tablespoons of ground ginger. Stir in the water and sprinkle over the yeast. Leave in a warm place until the yeast has dissolved, then stir well and cover loosely. Leave to stand in a warm place for two weeks, feeding the plant each day with 1 teaspoon each of honey and ginger. Stir well each time and keep covered.

At the end of two weeks, strain the ginger beer plant through muslin or fine cotton. Squeeze out all the liquid and place it in a 4.5-litre/1-gallon container. Stir in the honey, sugar and lemon juice, then make up to 4.5 litres/1 gallon with cold water.

Pour into clean strong bottles and cover with caps – screw these down only loosely or the ginger beer will become too fizzy. Store in a cool place for a week when it will be ready to drink.

The residue from straining the ginger beer plant should be divided in half and each portion placed in a large jar. Top them up with 300 ml/½ pint water and feed with honey and ginger as before. If you don't want to make gallons of ginger beer give one of the plants to a friend.

Banana and Honey Shake

Milk drinks are particularly nutritious and useful to give children who are off their food. Both adults and children alike will appreciate this drink on a hot day. For a special treat, serve a scoop of ice cream in the glass. Serves 2–3

Metric		Imperial
2	bananas	2
2 tablespoons	clear honey	2 tablespoons
300 ml	milk	½ pint
2	ice cubes	2

Slice the bananas into a liquidiser. Add the honey and milk and blend until smooth. Pour into individual glasses and float an ice cube in each. Place a couple of drinking straws in each glass and serve.

Honey-mulled Cider

A mixture of honey and spices, with just a little rum, turns an inexpensive bottle of cider into a special occasion drink. Serves 6

Metric		Imperial
1	orange	1
12	cloves	12
2	cinnamon sticks	2
4–6 tablespoons	clear honey	4–6 tablespoons
4 tablespoons	dark rum	4 tablespoons
	dash of lemon juice	
1.15 litres	dry cider	2 pints
1	dessert apple, cored and sliced	1

Stud the orange with the cloves and place it in a saucepan. Add the cinnamon sticks and honey and pour in the rum. Stir in the lemon juice and cider, then leave over very low heat for about an hour. Add the apple slices and serve very warm.

Note: To keep mulled drinks and punches warm, place them in a heatproof bowl over a plate warmer. Alternatively, serve the drink from an attractive flameproof casserole placed over a fondue burner.

Sparkling Cooler

Serve this light and fruity sparkling drink to make your party go with a real zing! To make the punch slightly less potent add a small bottle of tonic water before serving. Serves 6

Metric		Imperial
	juice of 4 oranges	
4 tablespoons	clear honey	4 tablespoons
150 ml	brandy	$\frac{1}{4}$ pint
1	bottle dry sparkling white wine	1
$\frac{1}{4}$	cucumber, thinly sliced	$\frac{1}{4}$
1	orange, thinly sliced	1
	ice	

Mix the orange juice with the honey and brandy. Pour in the sparkling wine and add the cucumber and orange slices. Stir in plenty of ice and serve in tall glasses.

Honey Glogg

A glass of this full-flavoured punch will produce a warm glow deep inside even on the coldest of evenings. Serves 6

Metric		Imperial
50 g	blanched almonds	2 oz
50 g	raisins	2 oz
6	cloves	6
1	cinnamon stick	1
2	cardamoms	2
6 tablespoons	clear honey	6 tablespoons
1	bottle dry red wine	1
150 ml	brandy	$\frac{1}{4}$ pint

Cut the almonds into slivers and place them in a saucepan with the raisins, spices and honey. Pour in the wine and leave over very gentle heat for about an hour. Do not let the wine boil and give it the occasional stir.

Separately, warm the brandy very slightly. Pour the glogg into a heatproof serving bowl and pour over the brandy. Ignite immediately and serve while still flaming.

Bee Sting

Here's a drink with a bite on its tail! Short and very strong, serve this cocktail only to those you know can take it. The flavour is superb and the warm glow that follows in the wake of just a couple of sips is very pleasing. Serves 2

Metric		Imperial
1	sherry glass dark rum	1
1	sherry glass dry vermouth	1
1 tablespoon	clear honey	1 tablespoon

Mix all the ingredients together in a small jug and chill thoroughly. Serve with ice, in small cocktail glasses – if you feel strong, double the quantities.

Honey Blonde

Here's a tall slim cocktail for warm evenings. Serves 2

Metric		Imperial
2 tablespoons	clear honey	2 tablespoons
4	sherry glasses orange juice	4
4	sherry glasses dry sherry	4
2	sherry glasses dry vermouth	2
	ice and orange slices	

Mix the honey with the orange juice, stirring well to make sure the honey dissolves. Stir in the sherry and vermouth then pour the drink into two tall glasses and add plenty of ice. Decorate with a slice of orange and serve.

Honey Blackcurrant Drink

This delicious drink is full of goodness, ideal for growing youngsters and always useful in the fight against colds and flu. Makes enough syrup for about 12–15 drinks

Metric		Imperial
450 g	blackcurrants (fresh or frozen)	1 lb
450 g	clear honey	1 lb

Remove the stalks from the blackcurrants and make sure the fruit is clean. Place it in a bowl and pour over the honey. Crush the fruit with the honey – a potato masher is useful for this – then cover the bowl and leave it overnight. Crush the fruit several times, until all the juice has been extracted from it.

Press the fruit through a sieve, then pour the blackcurrant and honey mixture into a bottle. Store in the refrigerator. Dilute with cold water for a vitamin-giving drink.

Note: As well as making a refreshing drink, this fruit syrup can be poured over ice cream, used to flavour desserts or simply taken by the spoonful to ensure a daily supply of vitamin C.

Hot Honey and Lemon

Here is a warming drink to help soothe away sore throats and ease chesty coughs. Children will love it and adults will feel comforted by this beneficial brew. Serves 1

Metric		Imperial
	juice of ½ lemon	
2 tablespoons	set honey	2 tablespoons
	boiling water	

Mix the lemon juice and honey in a mug. Gradually pour in the boiling water, stirring to dissolve the honey, until the mug is almost full. Drink as hot as you can – remember to allow it to cool slightly for children though.

Note: When your throat is really sore, try slowly swallowing a couple of spoonfuls of the following old-fashioned soothing mixture – 2 teaspoons glycerine, 2 teaspoons clear or set honey and 2 teaspoons cider vinegar.

Hot Whisky Toddy

For adults, the only possible consolation in having a cold is being able to curl up in bed or in front of the fire with a heart-warming whisky toddy. Old-fashioned it may be but this drink certainly helps to induce sleep and ease all those horrid cold symptoms. Serves 1

Metric		Imperial
	juice of 1 lemon	
2–3 tablespoons	set honey	2–3 tablespoons
	boiling water	
3 tablespoons	whisky	3 tablespoons

Mix the lemon juice and honey in a large mug. Top up with boiling water, stirring to dissolve the honey, and add the whisky. Drink immediately.

Note: Gargling is an old-fashioned way of washing or rinsing out the throat. Soothing concoctions were meant to rinse away the cold poisons from the throat; by coating a sore throat with this mixture you can, in fact, help to ease away the pain. Mix 2 tablespoons set honey with 4 tablespoons cider vinegar and a pinch of salt. Gargle with, but do not swallow, the mixture.

Hot Honey Chocolate

As a nightcap or mid-morning pick-me-up, this drink is satisfying and relaxing. Makes 1 drink

Metric		Imperial
250 ml	milk	8 fl oz
1–2 teaspoons	cocoa powder	1–2 teaspoons
2–3 teaspoons	clear or set honey	2–3 teaspoons
1	chocolate flake	1

Heat the milk to boiling point, pour into a mug and, stirring continuously, sprinkle in the cocoa. Stir in the honey and stand a chocolate flake in the drink. Serve straightaway.

Beauty Preparations

Our daily routines take a lot out of our skin and hair. The wind and weather, harsh shampoos and soaps, creams and make-up, tints and perms, all gradually drain away the natural bloom and beauty. In addition, rushing around and worrying doesn't help – so often one feels tired and too often it shows. At some time or other it is a good idea to try and put back into our faces a little of the goodness that has been drawn out – for even the toughest of skins needs some attention.

The potions in this chapter are full of natural goodness; they are made from ingredients which will care for your skin, with no added chemicals or preservatives. Make them when you wish to use them, or keep them for a short time in small pots in the refrigerator. When you apply a face pack allow a little time for yourself – spend an hour alone, untroubled, relaxed and warm. It may sound like an impossible dream – particularly to a busy mother – but this occasional break will work wonders for your looks, your temperament and your ego!

Using a Face Pack

If possible, try and devote a short time every week to giving your face a little extra attention. Start by cleansing your face in the normal way or try cleaning your skin with honey; smooth a little warmed, clear honey over your face and leave it for 15 minutes. Wash off with warm water. You will find that this helps to draw out any blackheads to leave your skin clear and smooth. If your face is particularly blemished, mix the honey with a little wheat germ.

Another method of cleansing the face is to hold your head over a bowl of very hot water. Cover your head and the bowl with a towel and allow the steam to draw out the dirt. Just 10 or 15 minutes will leave your face feeling much cleaner. Scent the water first, if you like, with 1 tablespoon clear or set honey and some fresh herbs – mint or rosemary, for example. Add the rind of a lemon to the bowl for a particularly fresh scent.

When your skin feels clean, brush back your hair and spread on the face pack, then relax. Lie down with your feet slightly higher than your head and make yourself perfectly comfortable. Wash off the pack with warm water, then close the pores, if necessary, with a mild astringent. A little witch hazel and rosewater will do this very well. Try not to apply make-up for a short while after you have given yourself a face mask treatment.

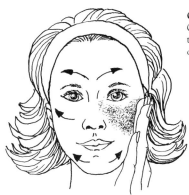

Cleansing your face with honey
Gently smooth warm honey over the face in an upward and outward direction.

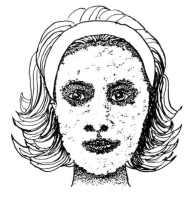

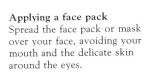

Applying a face pack
Spread the face pack or mask over your face, avoiding your mouth and the delicate skin around the eyes.

Oatmeal Face Pack

Use this pack regularly on dry or dull skin. Mix an egg yolk with 2 tablespoons clear honey. Mix in enough fine oatmeal to make a paste – the mixture should be firm enough to spread on your face. Smooth the pack gently over your skin, working from the neck upwards. Lie down and relax for 15 minutes then wash the pack off with lukewarm water and pat dry.

Lemon Face Pack

Allow about 20 minutes for this pack to clean and sooth oily skin or oily patches on your face. Mix 1 tablespoon set honey with 1 tablespoon lemon juice and the white of an egg. Whisk the mixture into a smooth cream. Spread or brush the pack on to your face, gradually building up a good covering. Use a soft, clean blusher or make-up brush for this if you like. Rinse off with cool water and pat dry.

Avocado Face Pack

This mixture will make dry skin feel very luxurious. Peel and mash half a ripe avocado pear. Mix in 2 teaspoons set honey and 1 teaspoon single cream. Smooth the mask gently over your face and neck. Leave for 10–15 minutes, then rinse off with warm water. This will leave your face feeling soft and smooth.

Egg White Pack

A simple mixture of egg white, lemon, honey and a little almond oil will whiten your skin and help to fade a stale suntan. Stir 1 tablespoon set honey with 1 teaspoon lemon juice and ½ teaspoon sweet almond oil. Add 1 egg white and stir in enough fine flour to make a smooth paste – not too thick, but creamy enough to stay on your face. Spread the mixture gently over your face and neck, then relax for about half an hour. Rinse off with warm water.

Parsley Mask

This is ideal for oily skin. Thoroughly wash and dry a handful of fresh parsley. Cut off the stalks and chop the rest very finely. Place the parsley in a mortar or small bowl and crush it with a pestle or wooden spoon. Mix in 1 tablespoon set honey and spread or brush the mixture over your skin. Leave for 20–30 minutes and rinse off with warm water.

Cool Cucumber Mask

Mix 1 teaspoon set honey with $\frac{1}{2}$ teaspoon witch hazel and 2 teaspoons chilled milk. Finely grate a 2.5-cm/1-in piece of cucumber and stir it into the mixture. Add enough dried milk powder to make a thin cream which you then spread over your face. Leave for 15 minutes before washing off the pack with cool water. This mask will awaken and refresh you – it is perfect for using at the end of a busy day before the evening begins.

Honey Hair Treatment

Mix 3 tablespoons clear honey with 1 tablespoon olive oil. Make sure the oil and honey are thoroughly mixed. Wash your hair in the normal way and towel dry. Massage the honey and oil thoroughly into the hair and wrap your head in a warm towel. Alternatively, warm your hair with a dryer for 20 minutes. Rinse your hair with warm water and wash it with a good shampoo. This treatment is good for dry or damaged hair. If your hair is suffering from the after effects of an unsuccessful perm, then this mixture will help to replace the shine and natural oils.

Honey Hand Cream

Mix 100 g/4 oz softened lard with 2 egg yolks, 1 tablespoon clear or set honey, 1 tablespoon ground almonds and a few drops of rosewater. Massage this cream into sore and chapped hands.

For removing stains such as those left by blackberries, first clean the hands with a mixture of lard and granulated sugar. Rub a generous coating of lard over your hands, then rub your hands together with plenty of granulated sugar. Carry on rubbing your hands for some time – the sugar will help to clean off the stains. Wash off the mixture with soapy water.

Index

Index

Index